Study Guide for TECHNICAL ANALYSIS OF THE FINANCIAL MARKETS

Study Guide for

TECHNICAL ANALYSIS OF THE FINANCIAL MARKETS

A COMPREHENSIVE GUIDE TO TRADING METHODS AND APPLICATIONS

JOHN J. MURPHY

NEW YORK INSTITUTE OF FINANCE

NEW YORK • TORONTO • SYDNEY • TOKYO • SINGAPORE

NEW YORK INSTITUTE OF FINANCE
NYIF and NEW YORK INSTITUTE OF FINANCE
are trademarks of Executive Tax Reports, Inc.,
used under license by Penguin Putnam Inc.

Formerly published as *Study Guide for Technical Analysis of the Futures Markets* (NYIF, 1987).

Portions of this book were previously published as *Technical Analysis of the Futures Markets* (New York Institute of Finance, 1985).

Printed in the United States of America

20 19 18 17 16 15

ISBN 0-7352-0065-3

Contents

How to Use This Workbook

This self-study manual has been designed and prepared by the New York Institute of Finance, with the cooperation and input of John J. Murphy.

This workbook is to be used exclusively with John J. Murphy's *Technical Analysis of the Financial Markets* (referred to as the "text").

The workbook's objective is to test—and thereby to ensure—your comprehension of the large body of knowledge associated with technical analysis.

The methodology is simple to follow and uses your time efficiently. Here are the recommended steps:

- Before reading the textbook, go to Lesson One in the *Study Guide* (page 1). There you will find the Reading Assignment, which for the first lesson is Chapters 1 and 2 of the text. You will also find a set of reading Objectives and a Reading Orientation, which give your reading focus and direction. Also note the list of Key Terms (page 2). Following each term is a page reference indicating where in the text you can find a definition or explanation of the term. Pay special attention to these terms.
- Read the chapters assigned for the lesson. As you read, stay aware of the objectives and key terms. Ask questions of the text. Don't be afraid to underline what you feel is important—or make marginal notes.
- Go to the Challenge section of the lesson (starting on page 3). There you will find a Matching Quiz, Multiple Choice, and sometimes Fill-In questions. Answer the questions "closed book" as best you can.

- Turn to the Answer Sheet, and compare your answers against those given there. To "grade" yourself on these exams, divide the number of correct answers by the total number of answers and multiply the answer by 100. The result is your percentage right. Should your "grade" be lower than 65%, you should re-read the material for that lesson.

The purpose of this comparison, however, is *not* to give yourself a grade. Rather, it is to determine the areas where your comprehension is weak. Toward that end, each answer has a page reference to the text and a brief explanation of why the answer is correct. We suggest that you follow up these page references by re-reading the relevant sections of the text and making sure you understand the answer.

Once you have taken these steps for Chapters 1 and 2, proceed with Lesson Two, beginning on page 7.

This workbook has been produced with the utmost concern for accuracy and freedom from error. Nevertheless, we welcome your comments with regard to improvement.

New York Institute of Finance
Publishing Division

Study Guide for TECHNICAL ANALYSIS OF THE FINANCIAL MARKETS

LESSON ONE

Technical Analysis and the Dow Theory

READING ASSIGNMENT

Chapters 1 and 2 of the text.

OBJECTIVES

After completing this lesson, you should be able to:

Define the basic terms, concepts, and premises of technical analysis.

Distinguish fundamental from technical analysis.

Compare and contrast the Random Walk and Dow Theories.

READING ORIENTATION

Chapters 1 and 2 deal largely with the basis and background of technical analysis. As you progress in the course, you will see again and again the terms and concepts that are introduced in these chapters. For now, a general understanding of the basic terms is adequate.

Before reading the assignment, review the key terms on the next page. Look for them as you read. When you've completed your reading, go to page 3.

KEY TERMS

accumulation, 26
chartist, 10-12
confirmation, 27
correction, 26
day trading, 9
descriptive statistics, 18
distribution, 26
divergence, 27
Dow Theory, 27, 31, 32-33
efficient market hypothesis, 19-21
failure swing, 29-31
flow of fund analysis, 15
fundamental forecasting, 5-6
inductive statistics, 18
lines, 31
market action, 1–2
minor trend, 25-26
price action, 2
primary trend, 25-26
public participation, 26
Random Walk Theory, 19-21
secondary trend, 26
sentiment indicators, 15
statistical (quantitative) analyst, 11
technical forecasting, 5-6
technician, 10-12
timing, 6-7
traditional chartist, 10-12
trends, 25-30
trend trading, 10
volume, 27

CHALLENGE

MATCHING QUIZ

Match each term at the left with a definition at the right, by placing the number of the definition in the fill-in space next to the term. A definition may be used more than once. There are more definitions than terms. The first term has been matched for you.

A. __8__ **accumulation**	1.	Either the industrial or the Rail average gives the signal, not both.
B. _____ **chartist**	2.	Usually retraces 33% to 50%.
C. _____ **confirmation**	3.	Trading intraday changes, tic by tic.
D. _____ **correction**	4.	A reversal pattern.
E. _____ **day trading**	5.	Price, volume, open interest.
F. _____ **descriptive statistics**	6.	Study of the effect of supply and demand on commodity prices.
G. _____ **distribution**	7.	The Industrial and Rail averages give the signal.
H. _____ **divergence**	8.	Informed buying by astute investors.
I. _____ **Dow Theory**	9.	A secondary indicator that should expand in the direction of the trend.
J. _____ **efficient market hypoth.**	10.	Informed selling.
K. _____ **failure swing**	11.	Price behavior is "serially independent" and unpredictable.
L. _____ **flow of funds analysis**	12.	Presentation of data.
M. _____ **fundamentalist approach**	13.	Study of cash positions.
N. _____ **inductive statistics**	14.	Intermediate term trading.
O. _____ **market action**	15.	A pattern of successively rising or dropping peaks and troughs.
P. _____ **Random Walk Theory**	16.	Generalizing, projecting, and predicting on the basis of collected data.
Q. _____ **raw data for chartist**	17.	One who makes subjective judgments in analyzing market action.
R. _____ **technical analysis**	18.	Study of market action through charting, in order to forecast future trends.
S. _____ **technician**	19.	The pricing structure of commodities.
T. _____ **trend**	20.	Market action discounts everything.
U. _____ **trend trading**	21.	Makes use of computers to analyze price behavior.
V. _____ **volume**		

MULTIPLE CHOICE

Circle the letter of the correct answer. The first question is answered for you.

1. Which of the following is *not* a premise of the technical analysis?
   - **a.** History is repetitive.
   - **(b.)** Price action reflects market action.
   - **c.** Prices move in trends.
   - **d.** Any influence on market action is reflected in prices.

2. Which of the following is *not* true of the fundamentalist's approach to analysis?
   - **a.** The technical approach includes the fundamental method.
   - **b.** Market prices tend to lead fundamental indicators.
   - **c.** Fundamental analysis studies supply and demand.
   - **d.** Fundamental analysis studies market action.

3. In which way is technical analysis the same or similar in both futures and stocks?
   - **a.** Pricing structure.
   - **b.** Margin requirements.
   - **c.** Timing.
   - **d.** None of the above.

4. Which statement best describes the Random Walk Theory?
   - **a.** Past price movements are indicators of future movements.
   - **b.** Price changes cannot be predicted.
   - **c.** You can beat the market by buying many stocks at random.
   - **d.** Market prices discount everything.

5. Which statement best describes the Dow Theory?
   - **a.** Price changes may be used as indicators of future market action.
   - **b.** Each stock must be considered separately from trends in the averages.
   - **c.** Averages discount everything.
   - **d.** None of the above.

6. The average length of a minor trend is:
   - **a.** Less then 3 weeks.
   - **b.** A month or more.
   - **c.** About 3 months.
   - **d.** Under 6 months.

7. Which of the following is a Dow Theory premise?
   a. The market has four trends: up, down, sideways, and regressive.
   b. Averages need not confirm one another.
   c. Market action discounts everything.
   d. Reversals must be expected at any time, unless a trend gives definite signals of remaining in effect.

8. Which statement is not true of any trend, according to Dow Theory?
   a. It may consist of primary, intermediate, and near-term categories of price movement.
   b. It consists of three phases.
   c. It should be confirmed by volume.
   d. A trend is likely to reverse itself at any time.

9. Which of the following is a criticism of the Dow Theory?
   a. It does not capture any significant portion of a trend.
   b. It does not generate buying or selling signals.
   c. Its signals usually miss the start of a trend.
   d. It has not been around long enough for analysts to evaluate results.

10. In the following chart, which point(s) is (are) best described as a buy signal?

I. A, C, and E.	a. I only.
II. B1 and B2.	b. II only.
III. D.	c. II and III only.
	d. III only.

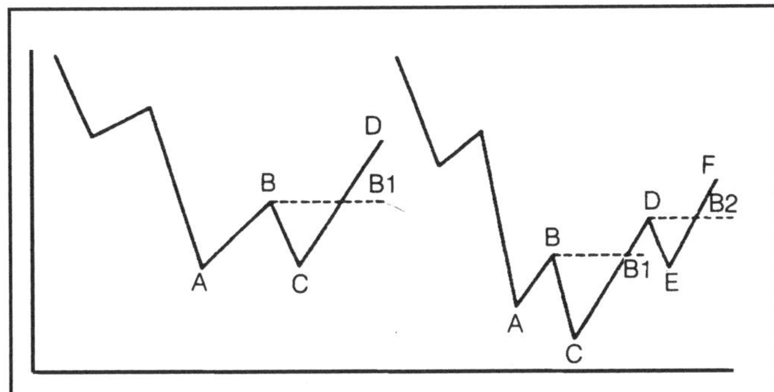

ANSWER SHEET

MATCHING QUIZ

A. 8	H. 1	O. 5
B. 17	I. 20	P. 11
C. 7	J. 11	Q. 5
D. 2	K. 2	R. 18
E. 3	L. 13	S. 21
F. 12	M. 6	T. 15
G. 10	N. 16	U. 14
		V. 9

MULTIPLE CHOICE

1. **b** See page 2 of the text.
2. **d** Fundamental analysis focuses on supply and demand underlying market action. See pages 5–6.
3. **d** See pages 5–6. More specifically, see pages 12–14.
4. **b** To see why answer b is rejected by technical analysts, see page 18.
5. **c** See page 24-25.
6. **a** See page 25-26.
7. **c** Answer a cannot be correct because Dow recognized only three trends (see page 21). Answer b is not correct (see page 27). Pages 28–29 explain why answer d is not true.
8. **d** See page 25-27 to see why answers a, b, and c are wrong. Pages 28–29 explain why answer d is not true.
9. **c** See pages 31–32.
10. **b** See page 31.

LESSON TWO
Chart Construction

READING ASSIGNMENT

Chapter 3 of the text.

OBJECTIVES

After completing this lesson, you should be able to:

- Identify bar, line, and point and figure charts.
- Read the information and identify the elements contained in a bar chart.
- Explain the basic elements of the candlestick.
- Distinguish volume from open interest.

READING ORIENTATION

This chapter introduces the basic charts of traditional technical analysis: bar, line, and point and figure charts. It also introduces the candlestick chart, which is explained further in Chapter 12 of the text.

KEY TERMS

arithmetic scale, 39-40
candlestick chart, 37-39
daily bar chart, 36, 40-41
intraday chart, 45
line chart, 36-37
logarithmic scale, 39-40
monthly bar chart, 35, 42-44
open interest, 35, 42-44
point and figure chart, 37,38
real body, 38
shadow, 38
volume, 35, 41-42
weekly bar chart, 35, 45-46

CHALLENGE

MATCHING QUIZ

A. __2__ daily bar chart
B. _____ intraday chart
C. _____ line chart
D. _____ open interest
E. _____ point and figure chart
F. _____ volume

1. All outstanding contracts at end of trading.
2. Presents day-to-day price action data by means of vertical rules in series.
3. Presents price action data by means of Xs and Os.
4. Presents market action data in terms of volume only.
5. Presents market action data by means of straight lines connecting plotted points.
6. All contracts traded during the day.
7. Presents price action for a period of less than one day.

MULTIPLE CHOICE

1. Which chart is used the most in futures technical analysis?
   - **a.** Point and figure.
   - **b.** Line chart.
   - **c.** Intraday chart.
   - **d.** Daily bar chart.

Refer the following charts for questions 2–5:

a.

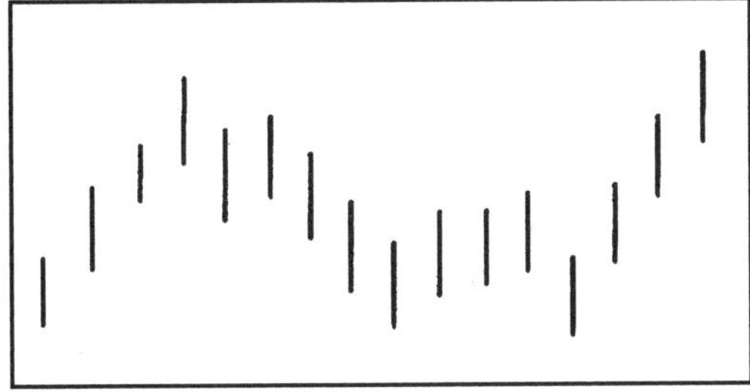

b.

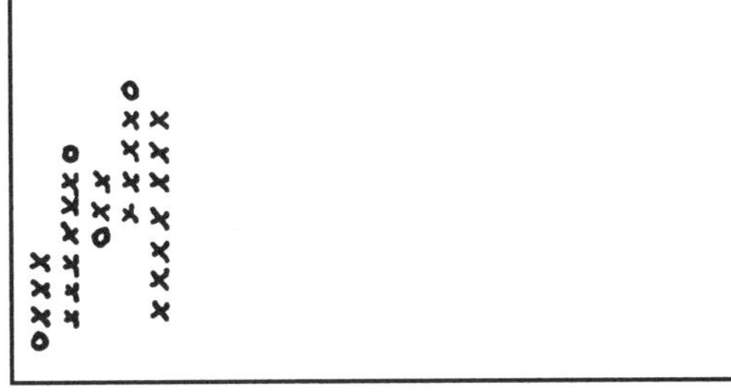

c.

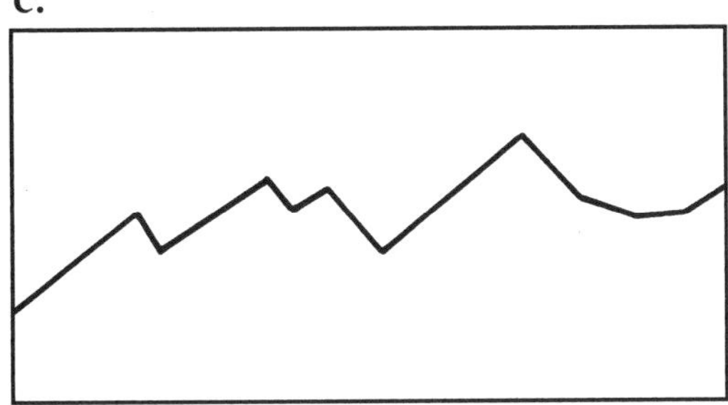

d.

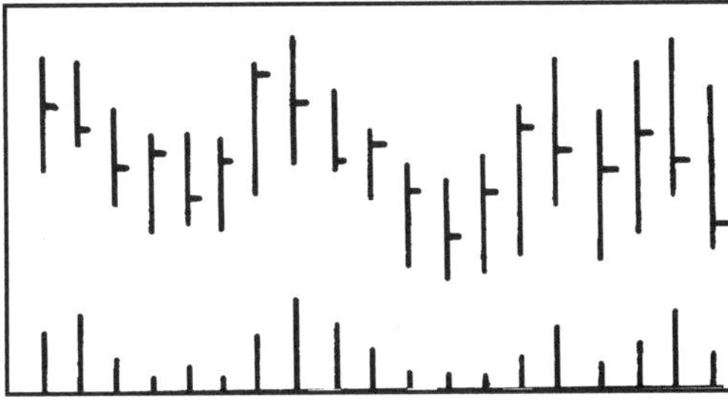

2. Which is a point and figure chart?

3. Which is a bar chart?

4. Which is a line chart?

5. Which reflects volume?

6. The horizontal tic to the right of a bar represents the:
   a. Average price for the day.
   b. Closing price.
   c. Opening price.
   d. Cumulative average price.

7. Which statement best defines *volume*?
   a. The total number of outstanding contracts held by market participants at the close.
   b. The total amount of trading activity in that commodity for the day.
   c. The total amount of trading activity in the commodities market in general.
   d. The total amount of trading activity as reflected in the Commodity Research Bureau Index.

8. Which statement best defines *open interest*?
   a. The total number of outstanding contracts held by market participants at the close.
   b. The total amount of trading activity in that commodity for the day.
   c. The total amount of trading activity in the commodities market in general.
   d. The total amount of trading activity as reflected in the Commodity Research Bureau Index.

9. Which statements are *true*?
   I. High open interest reflects high liquidity.
   II. High open interest reflects heavy trading.
   III. Buying or selling on high open interest is easier than on low open interest.

   a. I only.
   b. I and II only.
   c. I and III only.
   d. I, II, and III.

Refer to the following newspaper report and diagram for questions 10–15.

Crude oil, Light Sweet (NYM) 42,000 gal., $ per bbl.

	Open	High	Low	Settle	Change	Lifetime High	Lifetime Low	Open Interest
Jan	26.70	26.84	26.47	26.80	+.04	31.50	26.45	5,112
Feb	26.73	26.81	26.46	26.78	+.01	31.30	26.47	23,212
Mar	26.57	26.71	26.38	26.70	.....	31.45	26.37	16,343

10. For February crude oil, point I on the bar chart would be:
    a. 26.73
    b. 26.81
    c. 26.46
    d. 26.78

11. For January crude oil, point II would be:
    a. 26.70
    b. 26.47
    c. 26.80
    d. 31.50

12. For January crude oil, point III would be:
    a. 26.70
    b. 26.47
    c. 26.80
    d. 31.50

13. For March crude oil, point IV is:
    a. 26.38
    b. 26.70
    c. 31.45
    d. 26.37

14. The previous day's closing price for January crude oil was:
    a. 26.76
    b. 26.80
    c. 26.84
    d. Cannot be determined.

15. Which month has the greatest total number of outstanding contracts at the end of the day?
    a. January
    b. February
    c. March
    d. Cannot be determined.

16. On a candlestick chart, the shadow (a thin line) shows which of the following?
    a. The distance between the opening and closing prices.
    b. The range between the high and low.
    c. Whether the closing price is higher than the opening price.
    d. Whether the opening price is higher than the closing price.

17. On a candlestick chart, the real body (the wider portion) shows which of the following?
    a. The distance between the opening and closing prices.
    b. The range between the high and low.
    c. Whether the closing price is higher than the opening price.
    d. Whether the opening price is higher than the closing price.

18. On a candlestick chart, what does a white real body show?
    a. The distance between the opening and closing prices.
    b. The range between the open and close.
    c. The closing price is higher than the opening price.
    d. The opening price is higher than the closing price.

ANSWER SHEET

MATCHING QUIZ

A. 2
B. 7
C. 5
D. 1
E. 3
F. 6

MULTIPLE CHOICE

1. **d** Despite the fact that other types of charts are used (point and figure or longer-term bar charts), the daily bar chart is by far the most commonly employed (see page 36).
2. **b** Compare this chart with the one on page 38 of the text or Figure 11.5a on page 272.
3. **a or d** Compare either chart with Figure 3.1 (page 36) or Figure 3.7 (page 42).
4. **c** Compare this chart with Figure 3.2 (page 37).
5. **d** The vertical bars at the base of the chart reflect volume (see page 41-42).
6. **b** See page 40-41.
7. **b** Answer a is open interest (page 42). Answer c is not correct because, on a chart, volume refers to trading in the market being charted, not in the commodities market as a whole. Alternative d is out; volume on a chart has nothing to do with the CRB index.
8. **a** This definition comes right from the first paragraph of page 42. Answers b, c, and d have already been eliminated in the explanation for question 7.
9. **c** Alternative I is true, as explained on page 42-44. The second alternative is not necessarily true, since the number of outstanding contracts can remain high from one day to the next without heavy trading. For alternative III, again see page 42-44.
10. **b** Point I is the high for the day—that price is in the second column over from "Feb."
11. **a** Point II (the tic to the left of the bar) is the opening price for the day—the first price after "Jan."
12. **c** Point III (the tic to the right of the bar) is the closing price for the day—the number under the heading "Settle."
13. **a** Point IV is the intraday low. You'll find that number under the heading "Low."
14. **a** This number is not on the chart as such. To arrive at it, deduct the changes of +.04 from the present day's settle price: 26.80 less .04 equals 26.76. You deduct the +.04 because the change from yesterday was upward. If the number were negative, such as –.04, the change from yesterday would be negative; so you add the –.04.
15. **b** By definition, the "greatest total number of outstanding contracts" is open interest. If you look at the "Open Interest" figures for these contracts (last column), you see that the February contract has the highest open interest.
16. **b** See page 38.
17. **a** See pages 38.
18. **c** See page 38-39.

LESSON THREE

Basic Concepts of Trend

READING ASSIGNMENT

Chapter 4 of the text.

OBJECTIVES

After completing this lesson, you should be able to:

- Identify the directions and classifications of trends.
- Recognize support, resistance, and significant penetration.
- Understand the meaning of trendlines and channel lines.
- Perceive and interpret retracement and speedlines.
- Identify reversal days and gaps in price action.

READING ORIENTATION

The challenge section in this lesson is geared to test not only your understanding of, but also your ability to apply, the concepts in these chapters. While making up your own charts is neither suggested nor required, you will be asked to interpret patterns in several charts.

KEY TERMS

bottom reversal day, 91, 92
breakaway gap, 94-95
channel (return) line, 80-85
climax, 91
correction, 53
downtrend, 50-52
exhaustion gap, 96-97
intermediate trend, 52-54
internal trendlines, 90
island reversal, 97
major trend, 52-54
measuring (runaway) gap, 95-96
near-term trend, 42, 52-54
outside day, 92
price filter, 71-72
resistance, 55-56
retracement, 85-87
reversal, 56
reversal day, 90-93
sideways trend, 50-52
speedlines, 87-89
support, 55
tentative trendline, 67
time filter, 71
top reversal day, 91,92
trading range, 51
trendless, 51
trendlines, 65-74
two-day rule, 71-72
uptrend, 50-52
valid trendline, 67

CHALLENGE

MATCHING QUIZ

A. __17__ **bottom reversal day**
B. _____ **breakaway gap**
C. _____ **climax**
D. _____ **channel line**
E. _____ **correction**
F. _____ **downtrend**
G. _____ **intermediate trend**
H. _____ **internal trendline**
I. _____ **island reversal**
J. _____ **major trend**
K. _____ **measuring (runaway) gap**
L. _____ **near term trend**
M. _____ **outside day**
N. _____ **price filter**
O. _____ **resistance**
P. _____ **retracement**
Q. _____ **reversal**
R. _____ **reversal day**
S. _____ **sideways trend**
T. _____ **speedline**
U. _____ **support**
V. _____ **tentative trendline**
W. _____ **time filter**
X. _____ **top reversal day**
Y. _____ **trading range**
Z. _____ **trendless**
AA. _____ **trendlines**
BB. _____ **two-day rule**
CC. _____ **uptrend**

1. A pattern of descending peaks and troughs.
2. A flat, horizontal pattern.
3. Bottom reversal day.
4. Longer than a year.
5. Successive closes beyond the trendline.
6. Price action that is not in the trend's direction but that does not affect the direction of the trend itself.
7. Price will usually not go below this level.
8. A pattern of ascending peaks and troughs.
9. Measures the angle of a trend.
10. Period during which investors stay out of the market.
11. Reversal pattern with gaps before and after it.
12. Gap used to estimate the distance of a trend.
13. Three weeks to a few months.
14. Both the high and low on reversal day exceed those of the day before.
15. Prices have trouble rising above this level.
16. Change in a trend's direction.
17. Identifiable only after significant movement of prices in opposite direction.
18. To validate the breaking of a trendline, prices must close the trendline over or under for two successive days.
19. Two or three weeks.
20. Prices set a new extreme in the trend's direction during trading, but close in the opposite direction.
22. An intraday chart.
21. Gap that signals a significant market move.
23. In an uptrend, a bearish gap.
24. Needs a third point to be validated.
25. Two parallel lines containing the trend range.
26. Isolates valid penetrations by measuring the degree of price penetrations.
27. Does not rely on extreme high or lows, but is drawn through the price action.

MULTIPLE CHOICE

Refer to the following charts to answer questions 1–7:

a.

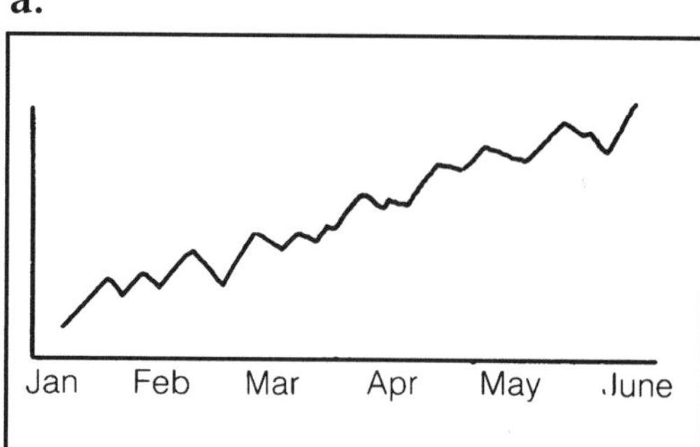

b.

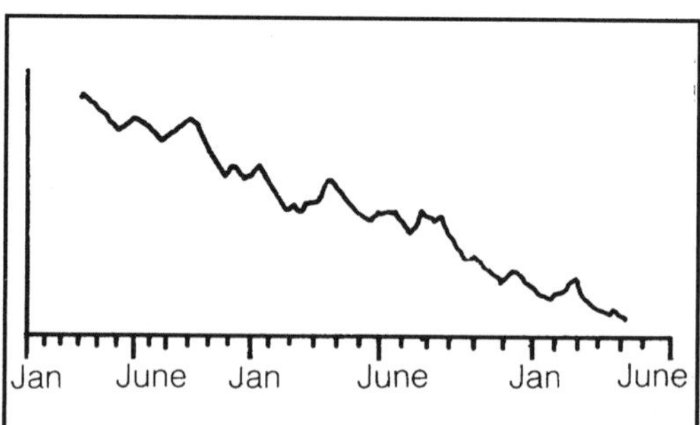

c.

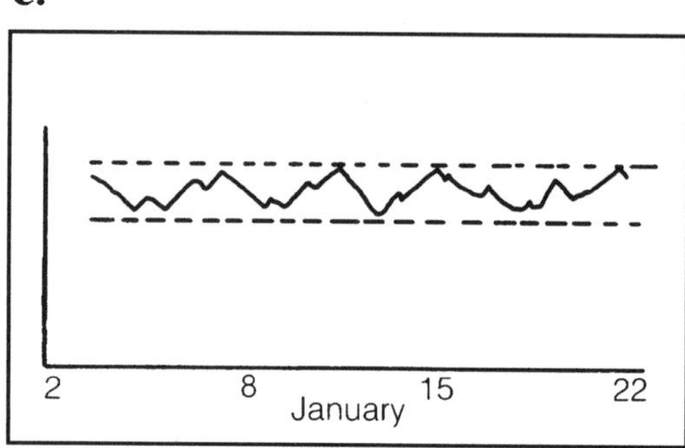

d.

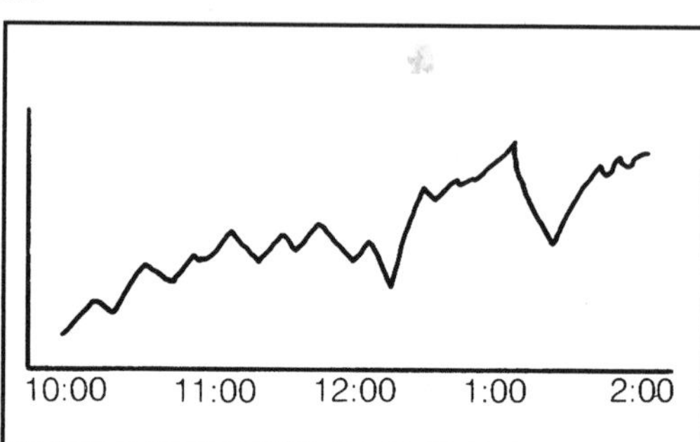

1. Which chart displays a sideways trend?

2. Which chart shows an uptrend?

3. Which chart is trendless?

4. In chart c, what do you call the area between the dashed lines?
   - **a.** Support zone.
   - **b.** Resistance area.
   - **c.** Trading range.
   - **d.** Retracement range.

5. Which chart shows intraday trading?

6. Which chart shows a situation indicating that staying out of the market is best?

7. At a support level:
   a. Buying pressure overcomes selling pressure.
   b. Selling pressure overcomes buying pressure.
   c. Buying and selling pressures stay equal.
   d. Prices turn downward.

8. Select the truest statement about resistance:
   a. It is a price level over the market.
   b. Buying pressure overcomes selling pressure.
   c. It cannot be penetrated.
   d. The chartist sets its level.

Refer to the following chart to answer questions 9–12.

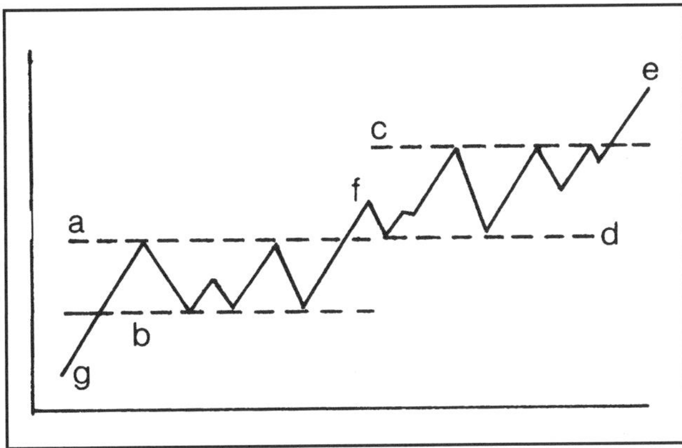

9. Which dashed lines represent support levels?
   a. a and c.
   b. b and d.
   c. a and b.
   d. c and d.

10. The principle shown by dashed line a–d is best described as:
    a. Continuous
    b. Corrective
    c. Role reversal
    d. Retracement

11. Which of the following does the chart *not* show?
    a. Support and resistance in an uptrend.
    b. Support and resistance in a downtrend.
    c. Trading ranges in an uptrend.
    d. A distinct uptrend.

12. Which solid lines clearly represent penetrations of resistance?
    a. e only.
    b. e and f only.
    c. e, f, and g only.
    d. None of the above.

13. Which is *not* a question to ask to gauge the significance of either support or resistance?
    a. How recent is the trading in the area?
    b. How heavy is the volume?
    c. How high is the open interest?
    d. How long have prices traded in this area?

14. With gold prices threatening to drop below $300 an ounce, you want to prevent a loss, but you wish to sell only in the event that the $300 level is penetrated. You should place a sell stop order at:
    a. A price slightly above $300.
    b. Precisely at $300.
    c. A price slightly below $300.
    d. A sell stop order is inappropriate for this purpose.

Refer to the following charts to answer questions 15–16.

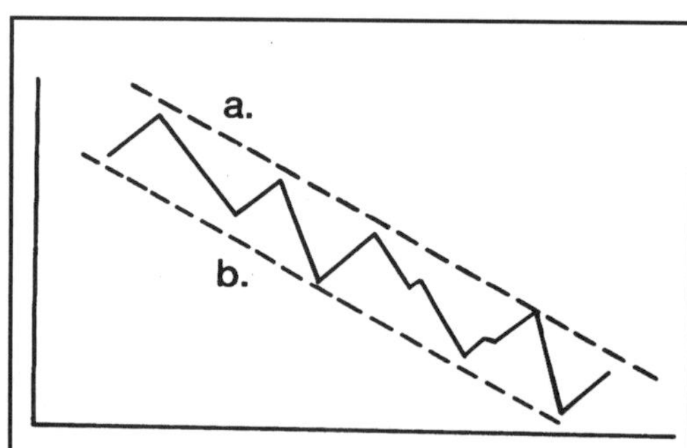

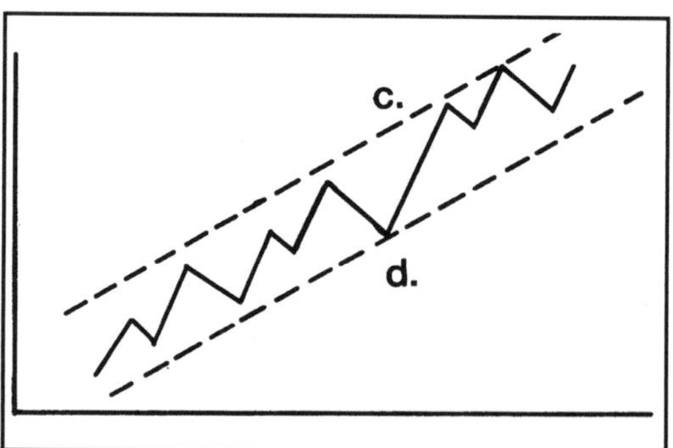

15. Which dashed line represents an up trendline?

16. Which dashed line represents a down trendline?

Refer to the following chart to answer questions 17–19.

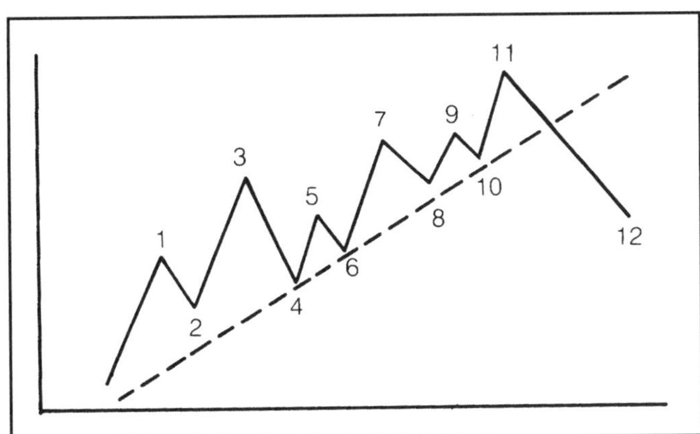

17. Which points in the trend may be used as buying areas?

a. 1, 3, 5, 7, 9, 11
b. 6, 8, 10
c. 2, 4, 6, 8, 10, 12
d. 5, 6, 7, 8, 9, 10

18. Which line(s) signal(s) a downside trend reversal?

a. 4, 6, 10, 12
b. 5, 9
c. 12
d. None.

19. Which is the least significant indicator of a trend reversal?

a. A penetration of the trendline of more than 3%.
b. A penetration two days in a row.
c. A closing price beyond the trendline.
d. An intraday penetration.

Refer to the following chart to answer questions 20–25.

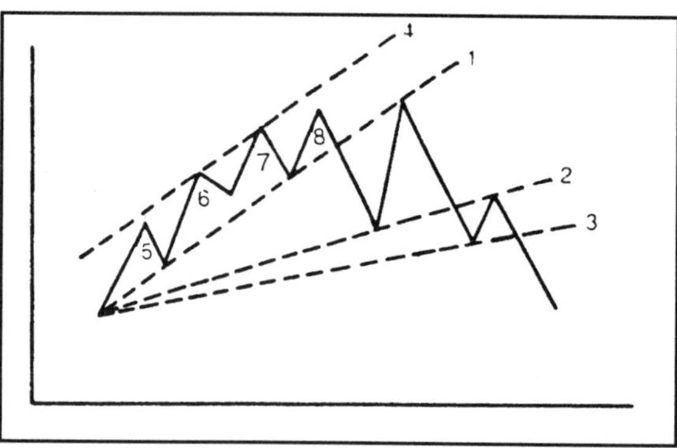

20. The trend is:
    a. Accelerating upward.
    b. Accelerating downward.
    c. Decelerating downward.
    d. None of the above.

21. The penetration of which line probably represents a trend reversal?
    a. 1
    b. 2
    c. 3
    d. 4

22. The chart is an example of:
    a. Head and shoulders.
    b. Fan principle.
    c. Retracement.
    d. Trading sideways.

23. Which line can be used for short term profit-taking?
    a. 1
    b. 2
    c. 3
    d. 4

24. Which point might represent a weakening trend?
    a. 5
    b. 6
    c. 7
    d. 8

25. If the difference between a channel line and a trendline has been $5 and an upward breakout occurs, prices will likely climb approximately how far above the channel line?
    a. $2.50
    b. $5.00
    c. $10.00
    d. Cannot be estimated.

Refer to the following chart to answer questions 26–29:

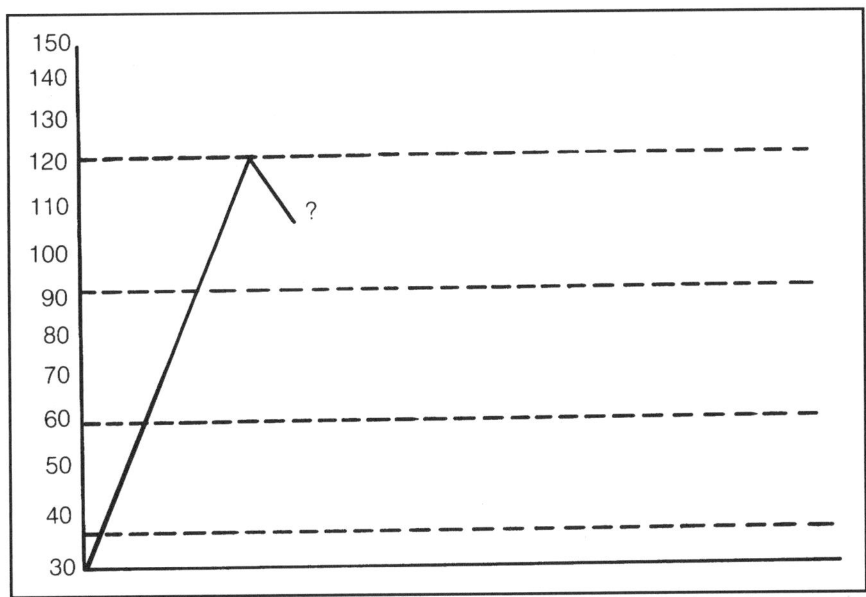

26. The downward-sloping line with the question mark represents a:
    a. Down trendline.
    b. Down tick.
    c. Retracement.
    d. Speedline.

27. If the line went down to the 60 level, the retracement would be:
    a. 33%
    b. 50%
    c. 66%
    d. 60%

28. If the line dropped below the 60 level, you should be thinking in terms of a:
    a. Trend reversal.
    b. Buying area.
    c. Sideways trend.
    d. None of the above.

29. If the line does *not* pass through the 90 level, you should be thinking in terms of a:
    a. Trend reversal.
    b. Buying area.
    c. Sideways trend.
    d. Short sale.

Refer to the following chart to answer questions 30–31:

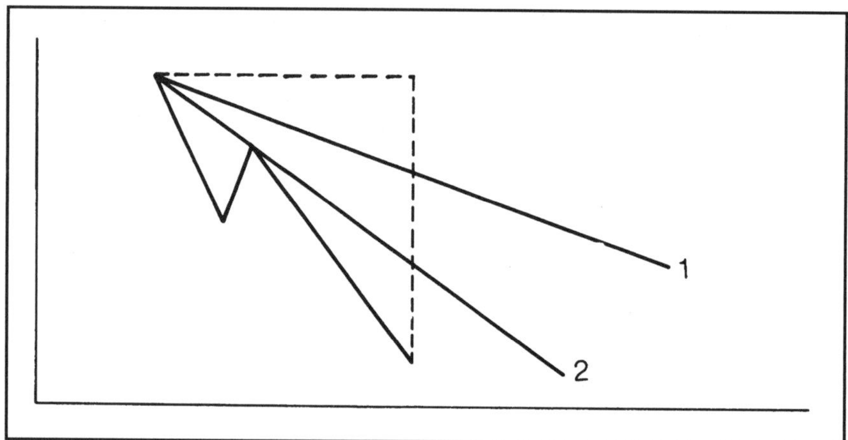

30. Lines 1 and 2 are:

  a. Retracement lines.
  b. Trendlines.
  c. Speedlines.
  d. Corrections.

31. Which is *not* true of line 1?

  a. It represents a retracement of 66%.
  b. It is "slower" than line 2.
  c. If prices break through line 2, they will probably rally to line 1.
  d. It may move through price action when being plotted.

Refer to the following charts to answer questions 32–34.

a.

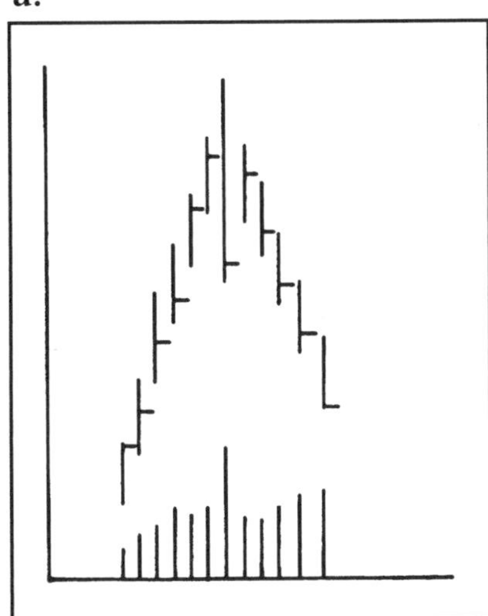

b.

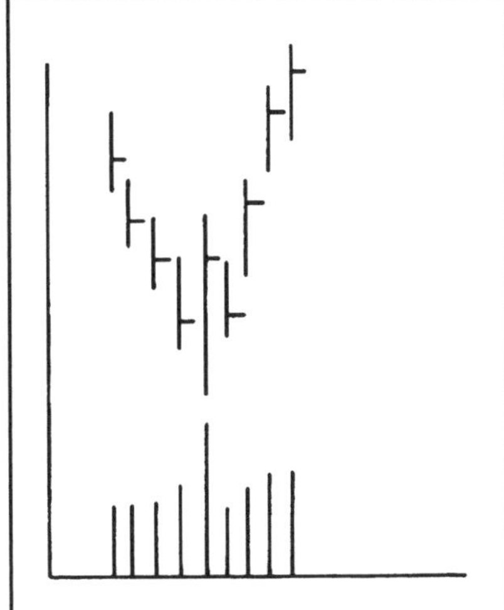

c.

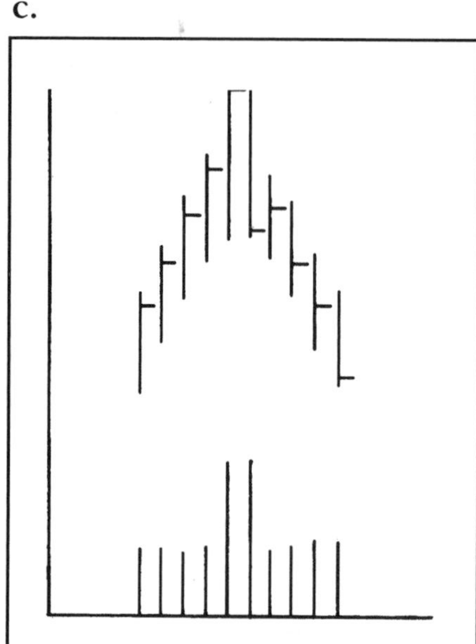

d.

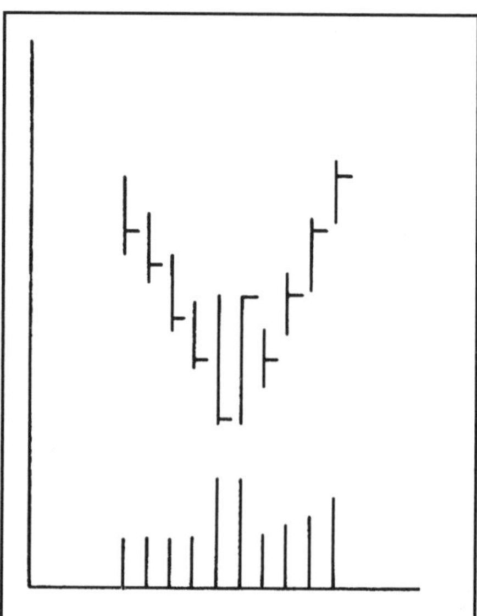

32. Which chart shows a top reversal day?

33. Which is an example of a two-day reversal bottom?

34. In all four charts, volume at each reversal point is:

a. Light.
b. Heavy.
c. Moderate.
d. Cannot be determined.

Refer to the following chart to answer questions 35–38:

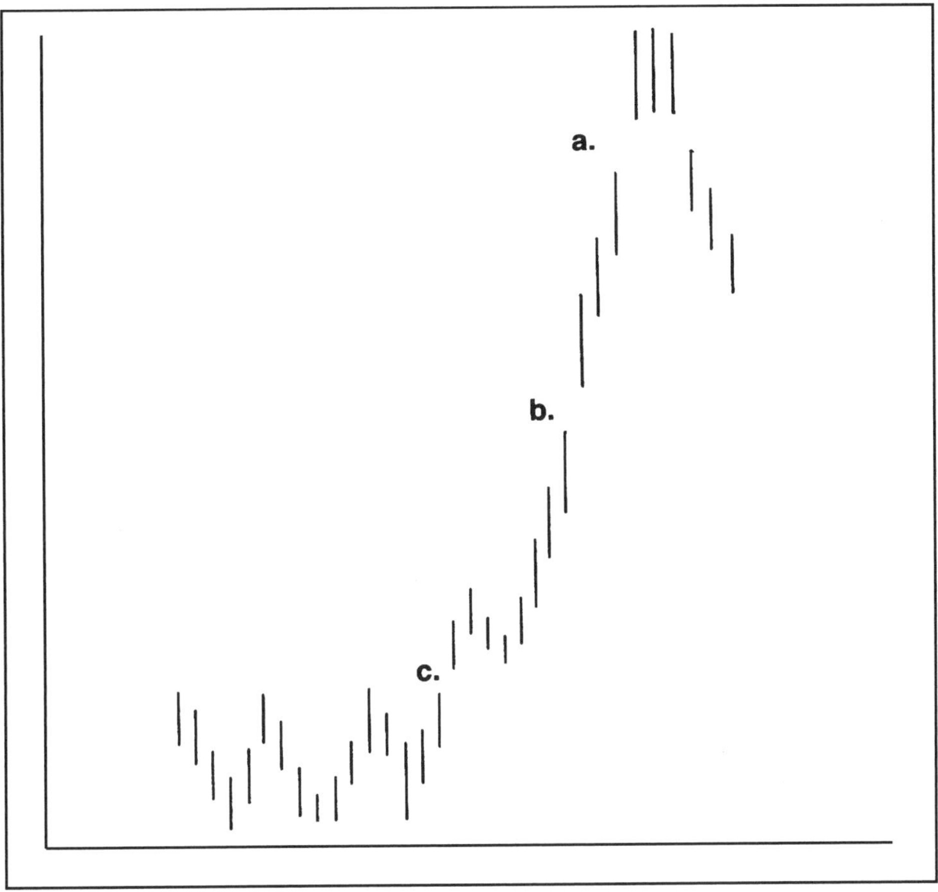

35. Which gap usually occurs on heavy volume and means that a price pattern has been completed?

36. Which gap usually occurs on moderate volume about halfway through a trend?

37. The filling of which gap has bearish implications?

38. The peak of this pattern is called a (an):
    a. Correction.
    b. Hidden gap.
    c. Island reversal.
    d. Downside breakaway gap.

ANSWER SHEET

MATCHING QUIZ

A. 17	K. 12	U. 7
B. 21	L. 19	V. 17
C. 3	M. 14	W. 18
D. 25	N. 26	X. 14
E. 6	O. 15	Y. 2
F. 1	P. 6	Z. 2
G. 13	Q. 16	AA. 9
H. 27	R. 20	BB. 18
I. 11	S. 2	CC. 8
J. 4	T. 9	

MULTIPLE CHOICE

1. **c** Compare this chart with Figure 4.1c on page 50.
2. **a** Compare this chart with Figure 4.1a on page 50.
3. **c** A market that moves neither up nor down, but rather sideways (or horizontally), is said to be trendless. (See page 51.)
4. **c** Support is an area below the market, and resistance is a level above the market (see page 55-56). Retracement is a countertrend (see pages 85-87). For an explanation of the correct answer, see page 51.
5. **d** "Intraday" means "within a day." The time calibration on chart d is in hours; the scales of all the other charts are in units of days, weeks, or months.
6. **c** This chart shows no trend. Is the market going to break out of the trading range upwards or downwards? It is almost impossible to tell on the basis of the chart above.
7. **a** Answers b and d are wrong because b describes resistance, which causes prices to turn downward. A support level reflects superior buying pressure, which turns prices upwards (see page 55). If buying and selling pressures are about equal (as in c), the market will move up and down within a narrow trading range, defined by a resistance level at the top and a support level at the bottom. See page 51.
8. **a** As for answer b, superior buying pressure constitutes support, not resistance (see page 55). Alternative c is wrong, since both support and resistance can be penetrated (see pages 61–63). The last statement, d, has to be wrong because the fundamental principle of technical analysis is that the market determines price levels; the chartist merely records them and interprets their movements.
9. **b** Compare these lines with those in Figure 4.4, pages 57-58.
10. **c** Once penetrated, support becomes resistance, and resistance becomes support. See pages 61–63. The terms "corrective" and "retracement" both refer to reversals in trend direction; the word "continuous" has to do with a trend's "continuing" in its present direction. None of the latter three terms has anything to do with support or resistance.

11. b First of all, the trend is distinctly upward, not downward, so answers a and d are incorrect. Further, trading ranges are defined between lines a and b and again between lines c and d; so alternative c is incorrect.

12. b Lines e and f clearly penetrate resistance areas indicated by lines a and c. No other lines do that. See pages 61–63.

13. c See page 60-61. Open interest is an indication of liquidity, not of buying or selling pressure.

14. c A sell stop *is* appropriate in this situation. Should prices dip below $300 and "set off" the sell stop order, you limit your loss. If you place it at or above $300, the order could be executed prematurely.

15. d The right-hand chart is one of an uptrend. Up trendlines are always drawn below the price action. Line c is a channel line. See Figure 4.6a on page 65 and Figure 4.17 on page 83.

16. a The left-hand chart shows a downtrend in prices. Down trendlines are always drawn above the price action. Line b is a channel line. See Figure 4.7b on page 69 and Figure 4.17 on page 83.

17. b Once an uptrendline is established (hence points 2 and 4 are not included in the answer), the buying points are whenever prices are near or at the support level (the dashed line). See page 68, particularly Figure 4.7a.

18. c The movement of prices to point 12 represents a significant breaking of the uptrend. No other low does that.

19. d See page 71. Clearly, a brief penetration during the trading day does not constitute a reversal.

20. b Note the angles of the trendlines 1, 2, and 3. Line 1 is pretty close to 45 degrees, a moderate upward rate. Lines 2 and 3 are progressively "flatter," indicating that the uptrend may be weakening. See pages 74–75.

21. c The breaking of the third trendline is a pretty sure indication that prices are headed downward. See pages 74–75, particularly Figure 4.11a.

22. b Compare the diagram with Figure 4.11a on page 74.

23. d The dashed line 4 is a channel line that runs parallel to uptrendline 1. Points 5, 6, and 7 reflect times to sell long positions or to enter short positions. See page 82.

24. d The peak at point 8 failed to test the channel line. See page 82.

25. b Usually the extent of the breakout is roughly the same as the width of the trading ranges before the breakout. See the bottom of page 82.

26. c The first alternative cannot be right inasmuch as it is not enough of a reversal to establish a downtrend. A "down tick" is just one transaction—at a lower price than that of the previous transaction. A speedline is a line that measures the rate of a trend, not part of the trend (see pages 87–89). Rather, this line represents a temporary reversal of an uptrend, or a retracement (see pages 85–87).

27. c The line would "retrace" 66% of the trend (see Figure 4.20a on page 86). The trend has endured from 30 to 120–90 points. If it drops to 60, that's a 60-point drop, or 66% (60 divided by 90).

28. a A retracement of more than 66% generally means the trend has reversed. In this case, buying would not be a profitable tactic, and the trend is certainly not sideways. See page 86-87.

29. **b** If prices turn upward again at 90, the retracement is 33%. (That's a 30-point drop divided by a 90-point trend.) The area between 90 (33%) and 75 (50%) is a good buying area (see page 86-87).

30. c Compare this chart with Figure 4.21 b on page 89.

31. **a** Line 1 is "slower" because its angle of descent is less; b is true. So is answer c (see page 87). Speedlines, unlike trendlines, may be plotted through price action (see page 85-86). Alternative a is not true; speedlines do not measure actual price retracement.

32. **a** See Figure 4.22a, page 92.

33. **d** See Figure 4.23b, page 96.

34. **b** Note how volume bars for reversal days are noticeably higher than on the days before and after the reversal. Heavy volume typically accompanies key reversal days. See page 92.

35. c This is a breakaway gap (see page 94-95).

36. **b** This is a runaway, or measuring gap (see page 95-96).

37. **a** This is an exhaustion gap (see page 96-97).

38. c Compare this chart with Figure 4.23a on page 95. See page 97.

LESSON FOUR

Major Reversal Patterns and Continuation Patterns

READING ASSIGNMENT

Chapters 5 and 6 of the text.

OBJECTIVES

After completing this lesson, you should be able to:

- Identify the five most commonly used major reversal patterns.
- Distinguish between reversal and continuation patterns.
- Identify continuation patterns such as triangles, flags, pennants, and wedges.
- Understand the importance of volume pattern and measuring implications.
- Read charts using price information.

READING ORIENTATION

In Chapters 5 and 6 you will study chart patterns. As will become evident, the patterns build on concepts discussed in the previous chapters. Central to Lesson 4 are the implications that price patterns have in forecasting transition periods. Therefore, price patterns can have predictive value when they appear on the price charts of commodities or stocks.

KEY TERMS

apex, 130
ascending triangle, 130, 131, 136-138
base, 130
broadening formation, 130, 140-141
bull trap, 122
complex head and shoulders pattern, 113-115
confirmation, 155-156
continuation head and shoulders, 153–155
continuation pattern, 100-101, 129-156
descending triangle, 130, 138-140
divergence, 155-156
double top or bottom, 100, 117-121, 122-124
flag, 141-145
flagpole, 143-144
head and shoulders top, 104-106
height, 102, 106-107, 118
inverse head and shoulders, 90, 110-112
maximum objective, 109-110
measured move, 151-153
measuring technique, 102, 118, 120-121
neckline, 104-106
pennant, 141-145
price objective, 108-110
price patterns, 100-103
rectangle formation, 147-151
return move, 106-107
saucer top or bottom, 125-127
spike top, 125-127
symmetrical triangle, 130, 131-135
triangle, 130-147
triple tops and bottoms, 115-117
volume pattern, 100
wedge, 119-120, 146-147, 148

CHALLENGE

MATCHING QUIZ

A. 10 apex
B. _____ base
C. _____ broadening formation
D. _____ bull trap
E. _____ complex head and shoulder pattern
F. _____ confirmation
G. _____ continuation head and shoulders
H. _____ continuation pattern
I. _____ divergence
J. _____ double bottom
K. _____ flag
L. _____ flagpole
M. _____ head and shoulders top
N. _____ inverse head and shoulders
O. _____ neckline
P. _____ pennant
Q. _____ price patterns
R. _____ rectangle formation
S. _____ return move
T. _____ saucer bottom
U. _____ spike top
V. _____ symmetrical triangle
W. _____ triangles
X. _____ triple top
Y. _____ volume
Z. _____ wedge

1. Often referred to as a "W."
2. The head is higher than either shoulder.
3. A false breakout.
4. Market advances or declines are divided into two equal and parallel moves.
5. A sideways price movement between two parallel horizontal lines.
6. Patterns where two heads or a double left and right shoulder may appear.
7. A market that is very hard to deal with because it happens so quickly.
8. A coil.
9. Preceded by a sharp almost straight uptrend.
10. Intersection point at the right where two trendlines meet.
11. Formations or pictures on price charts.
12. Pattern in which trendlines diverge.
13. Looks similar to a rectangle except for the middle trough.
14. A bounce-back.
15. In a triangle, the vertical line at the left that measures the pattern height.
16. Data that may help distinguish continuation or reversal patterns.
17. Used in determining minimum price objectives.
18. Where pennants and flags "fly at half-mast."
19. A pattern with a noticeable slant.
20. Generally a line with a slight upward slope at the top.
21. Continuation patterns of which there are three types.
22. Sideways price action that is a pause in prevailing trends.
23. A very slow and gradual trend change.
24. Technical indicators fail to confirm each other.
25. A method for arriving at price objectives.
26. Similar to a head and shoulders pattern, but with the peaks at about the same level.

Second column continued on next page.

27. When most indicators point in the same direction.
28. The opposite of the top pattern but usually accompanied by heavier volume.
29. Prices move sideways between two parallel trendlines.
30. A rare pattern whose peaks or troughs are about level.

FILL-INS

1. Measuring techniques help to determine the ________________ ________________ ________________.

2. In a head and shoulders top pattern, there are ________________ peaks.

3. In a valid head and shoulders top, once the neckline is broken, a subsequent close above the neckline is often called a ________________ ________________ ________________ ________________.

4. A symmetrical triangle represents a ________________ in the existing trend.

5. In an uptrend resumption, the ________________ in volume is essential in all consolidation patterns.

6. In a ________________ ________________, the two trendlines diverge.

7. The principal of ________________ is used to ensure that technical signals and indicators point in the same direction.

8. In a reversal pattern, ________________ is more important on the upside price breakout.

9. One of the most reliable and best known reversal patterns is the ________________ ________________ ________________.

10. A failure in confirmation of technical indicators is known as ________________.

MULTIPLE CHOICE

1. The following is not common of reversal patterns:
   a. The existence of a prior trend.
   b. The smaller the pattern the greater the subsequent move.
   c. Bottoms usually take longer to build than tops.
   d. All of the above.

2. The maximum objective is a:
   a. 100% retracement.
   b. 76% retracement.
   c. 0% retracement.
   d. 66% retracement.

3. In a "V" or spike reversal which of the following are true statements?
   I. It is a common pattern.
   II. The pattern is easily recognized.
   III. The market "turns on a dime."
   IV. It represents a gradual change.
   a. I only.
   b. II and III.
   c. I and IV.
   d. I and III.

Refer to the following figure to answer questions 4 and 5:

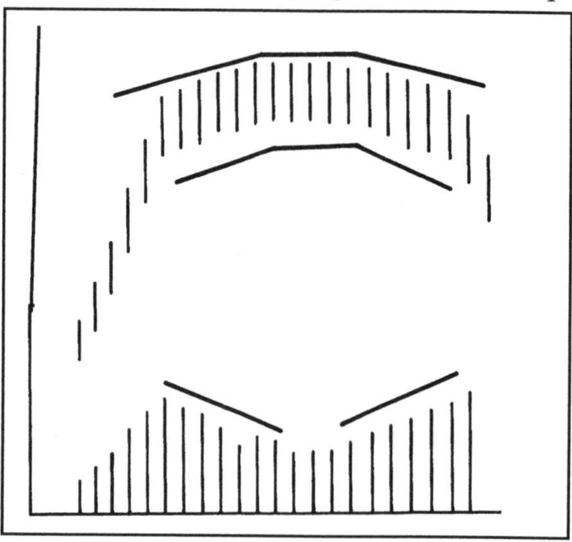

4. This is an example of a:
   a. "V" reversal.
   b. Saucer top.
   c. Nonpattern.
   d. Platter.

5. Which is *not* a true statement?
   a. This is a common pattern.
   b. It usually occurs at market bottoms.
   c. The trend change is slow and gradual.
   d. Volume diminishes at tops and bottoms.

6. Of the major reversal patterns the most common are:
   a. Head and shoulders, "V," and saucers.
   b. Head and shoulders, double tops and bottoms, and "V."
   c. "V," triple tops and bottoms, and the fan.
   d. Saucers, extended "V," and rectangles.

7. Which is *not* an example of a continuation pattern?
   a. Triangle.
   b. Rectangle.
   c. Pennant.
   d. Bowl, or saucer.

8. Which of the following is (are) characteristic of a head and shoulders top?
   a. Volume is important, as it is in all price patterns.
   b. Volume is more critical at market bottoms.
   c. Volume should probably increase for a new downtrend to continue.
   d. All of the above.

9. Which best describes continuation patterns?
   a. There is sideways price action.
   b. They take longer to build.
   c. They are representative of long-term patterns.
   d. These patterns always signal the onset of a new trend.

Refer to the following figures to answer questions 10–13:

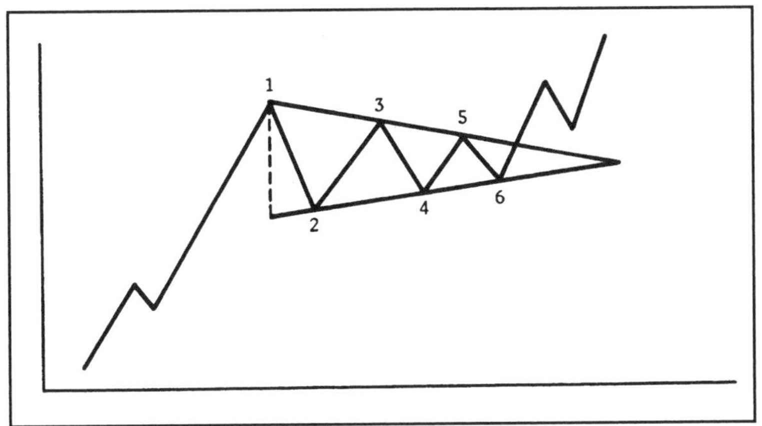

Figure I

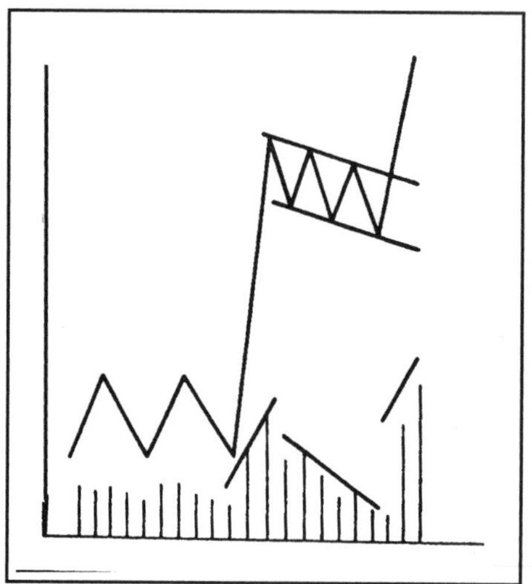

Figure II

Figure III

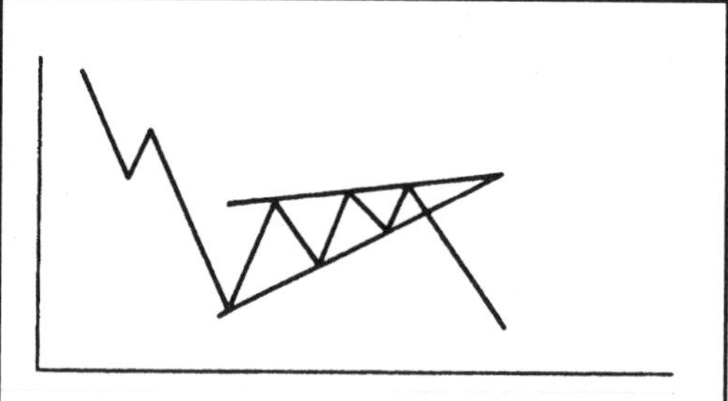

Figure IV

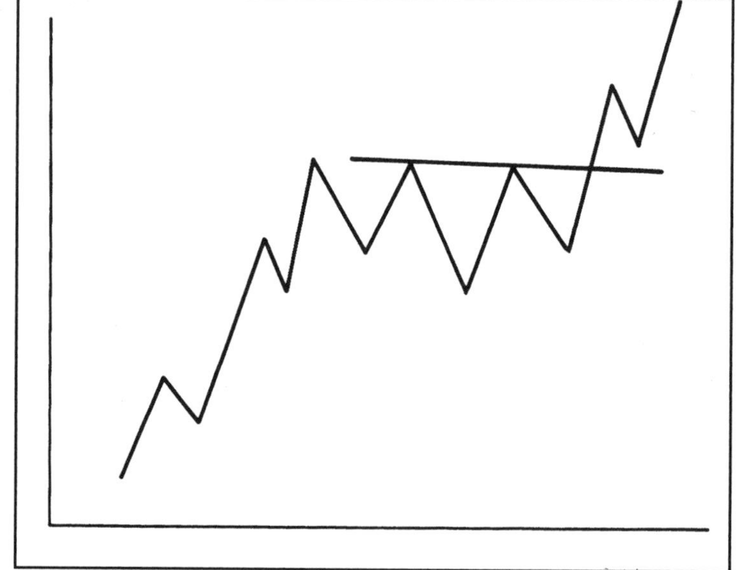

10. For this information pattern to occur a minimum of four reversal points is required.
    a. I
    b. II
    c. III
    d. IV

11. Which pattern is indicative of a bearish rising wedge?
   a. I
   b. II
   c. III
   d. IV

12. Which pattern(s) is (are) an example(s) of a bullish continuation head and shoulders?
   a. I and IV
   b. II
   c. IV
   d. II and III

13. Which pattern is preceded by a sharp line move?
   a. I
   b. II
   c. III
   d. IV

14. Which statement is true? In a valid double top:
   a. There are two distinguishable peaks at very different price levels.
   b. Volume is lighter during the first peak.
   c. Sometimes as many as four return moves occur.
   d. Height is often used as a measuring technique.

Refer to the following figure to answer questions 15 and 16:

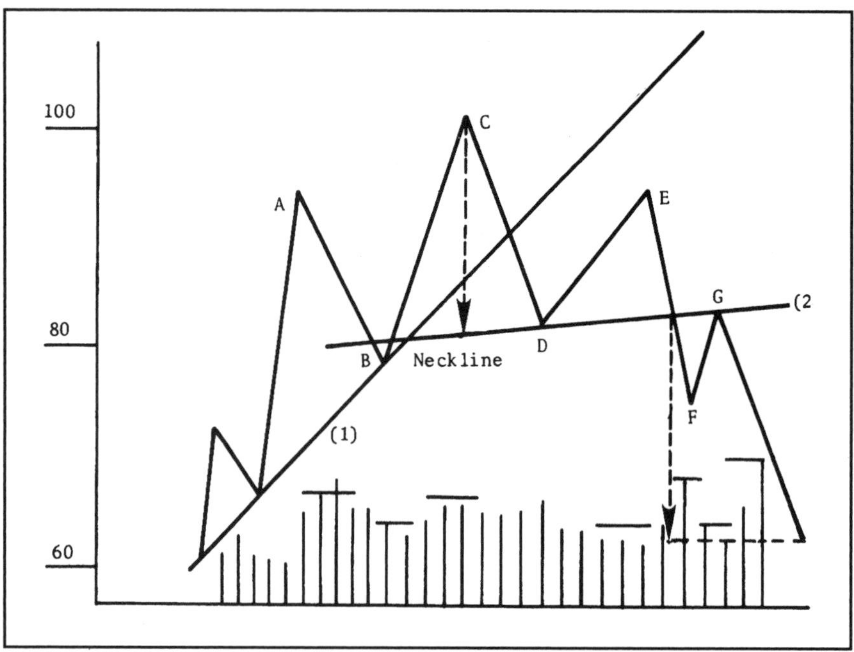

15. In this very common reversal pattern, the return move between F and G will:
    a. Occur on extremely high volume.
    b. Always exceed point E.
    c. Usually not recross the neckline once it's broken.
    d. Always be accompanied by a new trend.

16. This figure is an example of a:
    a. Head and shoulders bottom.
    b. Triple top.
    c. Double top.
    d. Head and shoulders top.

ANSWER SHEET

MATCHING QUIZ

A. 10
B. 15
C. 12
D. 3
E. 6
F. 27
G. 13
H. 22
I. 24
J. 1
K. 9
L. 18
M. 2
N. 28
O. 20
P. 9
Q. 11
R. 29
S. 14
T. 23
U. 7
V. 8
W. 21
X. 26
Y. 16
Z. 19

FILL-INS

1. minimum price objective
2. three
3. failed head and shoulders
4. pause
5. increase
6. broadening formation
7. confirmation
8. volume
9. head and shoulders
10. divergence

MULTIPLE CHOICE

1. **b** Common to all reversal trends is a need for a prior trend, the breaking of important trendlines, topping and bottom patterns—of which bottoms take longer to build, and the larger the price pattern the greater the subsequent move.
2. **a** The maximum objective is a 100% retracement of a previous bull market. The 66% retracement may provide significant support under the market. See page 109.
3. **d** This pattern is not uncommon. It is often marked by an abrupt reversal trend with little forewarning. It is also one of the most difficult patterns to recognize. See page 125.
4. **b** This figure is an example of a saucer top. It represents a slow gradual change in a trend. See page 125-126.
5. **a** This is a fairly infrequent pattern. B, C, and D are common characteristics of saucers. See page 125-126.
6. **b** In choices A and D, saucers are rare and the rectangle is usually a continuation pattern. There is no such thing as a fan in either reversal or continuation patterns.
7. **d** A "bowl" is another word used to describe a saucer that is a reversal pattern. See page 125.
8. **d** All of the statements are applicable to a head and shoulders top. See pages 104–106.
9. **a** Continuation patterns usually are short-term in duration, take shorter periods of time to build, and generally are only a pause in the prevailing trend. See page 129.

10. a This is an example of a bullish symmetrical triangle. See page 130-131. The minimum requirement for such a formation is four reversal points. However, most have six reversal points as shown in this figure.

11. c A falling wedge is usually bullish. It is characterized by two converging trendlines with the slope against the prevailing trend. See Figure 6.8a on page 146.

12. c This pattern is somewhat similar to a sideways rectangle except that the middle trough in the uptrend is generally lower than the two shoulders. See pages 153–154.

13. b This is an example of a bullish flag. It usually occurs after a sharp move and as continuation patterns go, this represents a pause in the trend. See page 142.

14. d There are two distinguishable peaks, but they usually are at similar price levels. Volume tends to be heavier on the first peak, lighter on the second. Several return moves would not be reflective of a valid top and head pattern. See page 118-119.

15. c If prices do recross the neckline, the technician should be alert to the possibility that a failed head and shoulders pattern exists. See page 153-154.

16. d This is an example of the classic head and shoulders top. This is the best known major reversal pattern. Most of the other reversal patterns are just variations of this pattern. An inverse head and shoulders pattern is the same, but it is "flipped on its head." See page 110-112.

LESSON FIVE

Volume and Open Interest

READING ASSIGNMENT

Chapter 7 of the text.

OBJECTIVES

After completing this lesson, you should be able to:

- Explain the importance of volume and open interest as secondary indicators.
- Explain the use of on balance volume (OBV).
- Read and understand the usefulness of open interest figures in the Commitments of Traders Report (COT).
- Understand how volume and open interest are used to detect trend changes.

READING ORIENTATION

The emphasis of this chapter is directed at helping the reader understand and recognize the importance of volume and open interest as trend indicators. With the conclusion of Chapter 7 the reader will have covered an essential and significant portion of the body of technical analysis.

KEY TERMS

blowoffs, 175
buyers and sellers, 160
Commitments of Traders Report (COT), 175-76
Commodity Futures Trading Commission (CFTC), 175
large hedgers, 176
large speculators, 176
liquidation, 173
on balance volume (OBV), 165-167
open interest, 159-162
put/call ratios, 178-179
selling climaxes, 175
small traders, 176
volume, 158-159

CHALLENGE

MATCHING QUIZ

A. __8__ blowoffs
B. _____ buyer and seller
C. _____ CFTC
D. _____ Commitments of Traders Report (COT)
E. _____ large hedgers
F. _____ large speculators
G. _____ liquidation
H. _____ on balance volume (OBV)
I. _____ open interest
J. _____ put/call ratio
K. _____ selling climaxes
L. _____ smaller traders
M. _____ volume

1. A three-month perpetual contract
2. Odd lotters.
3. Voluntary or involuntary close of a position.
4. Categorizes open interest by large hedgers, large speculators, and small traders.
5. A sudden price drop after a long market decline and large decline in open interest.
6. The total number of outstanding longs or shorts.
7. The number of entities being traded.
8. A sudden price rally and notable decline in open interest.
9. Granville's volume indicator.
10. Commodity Futures Trading Commission.
11. A contract must have both.
12. The most successful group in calling market turns.
13. A neckline slope.
14. Rely primarily on automated trend-following systems.
15. Helps to determine the bullishness or bearishness in an options market.

FILL-INS

1. ___________________ is the most important of the three indicators.
2. In a downtrend, declining open interest is ___________________.
3. The number of contracts traded during a specific time period is called ___________________.
4. ___________________ is a simple line indicator used to measure the volume pressure direction.
5. In open interest contracts there are groups of ___________________ and ___________________.

6. The total number of outstanding contracts is referred to as ____________ ____________.

7. For purposes of forecasting, only the ________________ volume and open interest are used.

8. Open interest can be affected in three ways. It can ________________, ________________, ________________ ____________.

9. If both parties liquidate old positions, then the open interest should ________________.

10. Open interest is accompanied by either a ________________ or ________________ number.

11. In an uptrend, rising open interest would be considered a ________________ sign.

MULTIPLE CHOICE

1. In general, if volume and open interest increase, then the current trend will:
   a. Usually continue in the same direction.
   b. Reverse.
   c. Signal an end to the current price trend.
   d. None of the above.

Refer to the following figure to answer question 2:

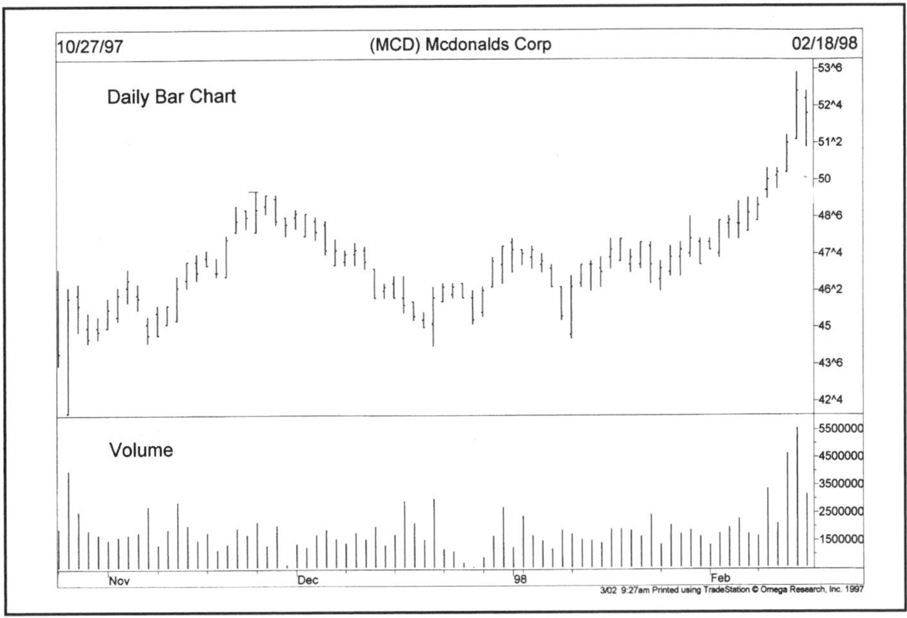

2. Which of the following statement(s) is (are) true?
   I. November of 1997 saw an upside price breakout.
   II. The breakout was accompanied by an increase in trading activity.
   III. There is heavy volume during December.
   IV. February 1988 saw an increase in trading volume.
   a. I and III.
   b. I, III, and IV.
   c. I, II, and IV.
   d. I, II, and III.

3. Volume is best considered:
   a. A primary indicator.
   b. A confirming indicator.
   c. A nonessential indicator.
   d. Useless if not compared to open indirect.

4. Declining open interest in a downtrend:
   a. Is bearish.
   b. Is bullish.
   c. Reflects a pause in the trend.
   d. Is very rare.

5. Which most accurately describes a danger signal at bull market tops?
   a. An unusually high open interest.
   b. Prices remaining in an uptrend.
   c. All longs have winning positions.
   d. None of the above.

6. Open interest increases when:
   a. A buyer buys new long and a seller sells old long.
   b. A buyer buys old short and a seller sells new short.
   c. A buyer buys new long and a seller sells new short.
   d. A buyer buys old short and a seller sells old long.

7. What does "volume precedes price" mean?
   a. There is no change in the buying or selling pressure.
   b. Pressure to sell is greater than pressure to buy.
   c. Price is less important than volume.
   d. Changes in the pressure to buy or sell are often detected in the volume before price.

8. What is OBV?
   a. Odd balance volume.
   b. On balance volume.
   c. Off balance volume.
   d. On balance variation.

9. What does it mean when OBV is used as an indicator?
   a. It is not a lead indicator for a price move.
   b. It never reflects divergence.
   c. It may be a confirming indicator.
   d. None of the above.

Refer to the following figure to answer question 10:

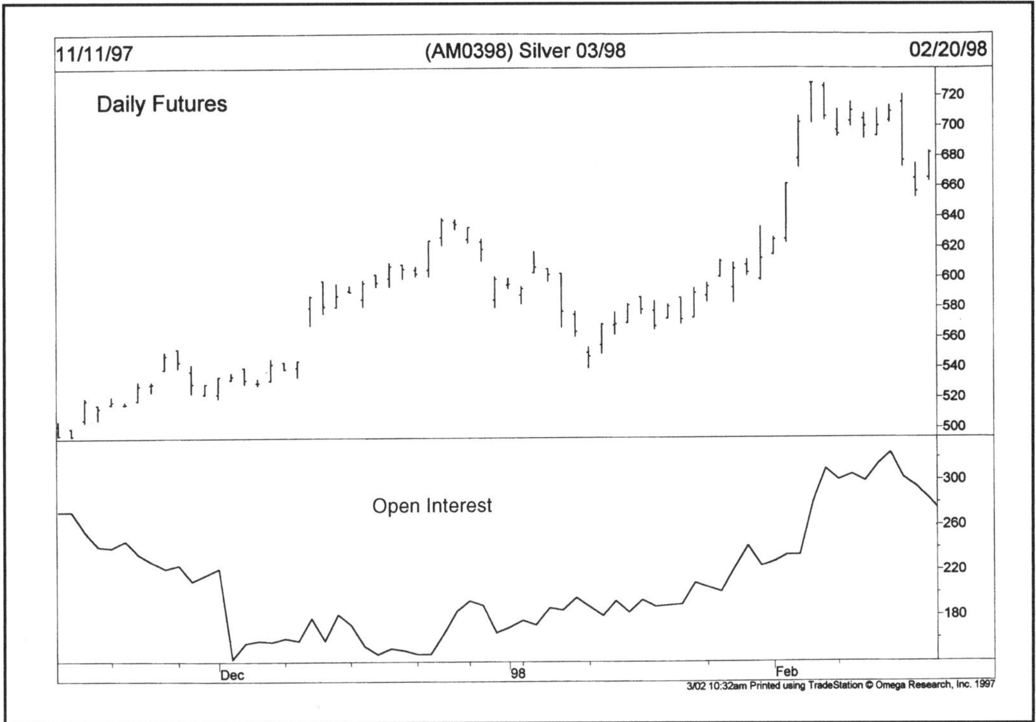

10. This figure shows:
    a. An overall downtrend in silver.
    b. An overall uptrend in daily futures.
    c. Liquidation during a February correction.
    d. Overall declining open interest.

11. The Commitments of Traders Report:
    a. Shows the open interest statistics of the previous month.
    b. Is released by the Commodity Futures Traders Committee.
    c. Is a new forecasting tool.
    d. Provides daily statistics.

12. Blowoffs are most prevalent:
    a. At major market tops.
    b. In sideways consolidation patterns.
    c. At major market bottoms.
    d. During slow trading.

13. Which is not true of a selling climax?
    a. Prices rise sharply first.
    b. There is heavy trading.
    c. There is a large decline in the open interest.
    d. Prices drop sharply.

14. Which group uses automated trend-following systems?
    a. Small traders.
    b. Large speculators.
    c. Large hedgers.
    d. Odd lotters.

15. The OBV line:
    a. Uses a plus or minus value.
    b. Is a volume indicator.
    c. Generally follows the direction of the price trend.
    d. All of the above.

16. Which of these individuals developed OBV?
    a. Marc Chaikin.
    b. James Sibbet.
    c. Joseph Granville.
    d. Charles H. Dow.

Refer to the following figure to answer question 17:

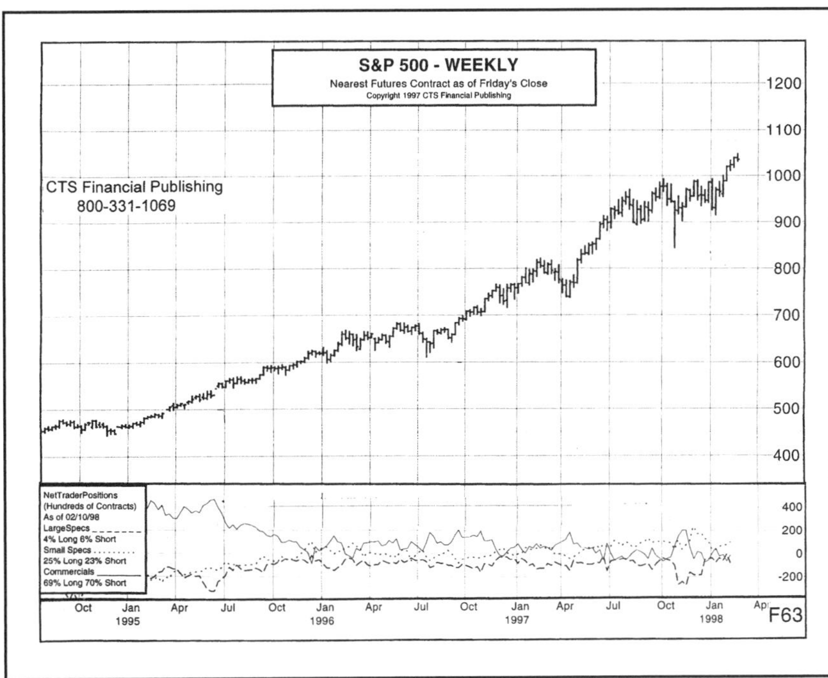

17. Based on the price action and net trader positions in the figure, how many buy signals do you see?

a. 1

b. 2

c. 3

d. 4

18. Open interest most accurately represents the:

a. Percentage of shorts and longs divided by two.

b. Total number of outstanding longs or shorts.

c. Difference between volume and seasonal tendencies.

d. One third of the preceding market move.

19. OBV lines attempt to determine whether heavier volume takes place on:
    a. Upside trends.
    b. Downside trends.
    c. Horizontal trends.
    d. A and B only.

20. Rising open interest in a downtrend is:
    a. Bearish.
    b. A poor indicator of market trends.
    c. Bullish.
    d. Reflective of sluggish new short selling.

ANSWER SHEET

MATCHING QUIZ

A. 8
B. 11
C. 10
D. 4
E. 12
F. 14
G. 3
H. 9
I. 6
J. 15
K. 5
L. 2
M. 7

FILL-INS

1. Price
2. bullish
3. volume
4. OBV
5. buyers ... sellers
6. open interest
7. total
8. increase, decrease, not change
9. decline
10. positive ... negative
11. bullish

MULTIPLE CHOICE

1. **a** *Declining* volume and open interest suggest that the present price trend may be ending. See page 161-162.
2. **c** Close inspection of this figure clearly shows light volume in December. See Figure 7-3 on page 162.
3. **b** See pages 163–164.
4. **b** Declining open interest in an uptrend is bearish, as is rising open interest in a downtrend. It does not reflect a pause in the trend nor is it a very rare occurrence. See pages 170-171.
5. **a** A high open interest figure at market tops may even be a bearish signal, especially if the price drop is sudden. See page 172-73.
6. **c** See the chart on page 160.
7. **d** Price is much more important than volume. There are definite pressures to buy or sell depending on the direction of the prevailing trend. See pages 163–165.
8. **b** On balance volume (OBV) is the only correct answer. See page 165-166.
9. **c** When it is used as a co-indicator, it can be a confirming or lead indicator of a price move. See page 167.
10. **c** See Figure 7.9 on page 170.
11. **a** It is not a new forecasting tool. It is a monthly, not a daily report. The CFTC is the Commodity Futures Trading *Commission* (not Committee). See pages 175.

12. a Blowoffs occur at major market tops. Prices generally rise sharply after long advances. There is a concurrent jump in trading activity and a notable decline in open interest. See page 175.

13. a Prices rise only after a sharp drop first. Selling climaxes occur at market bottoms. Selections B, C, and D are also true statements. See page 175.

14. b See page 176.

15. d All of the statements apply to OBV lines.

16. c Marc Chaikin developed the volume accumulation line. This is a sensitive intraday measure. Sibbet developed the Demand Index, which uses complicated formulas that incorporate volume with price action. Dow first published stock market averages; he is given credit for what is commonly known as the Dow Theory. His theory is the foundation of technical analysis. See page 165.

17. c See Figure 7.13 on page 178.

18. b Of the choices available, the most accurate statement is that open interest is the total number of outstanding shorts or longs. See page 160.

19. d The primary function of the OBV line is to determine whether volume is taking place on the upside or downside. See page 165.

20. a Rising open interest in an uptrend is a bullish sign. Rising open interest in a downtrend is also reflective of aggressive new short selling. See page 172-173.

LESSON SIX

Long-Term Charts

READING ASSIGNMENT

Chapter 8 of the text.

OBJECTIVES

After completing this lesson, you should be able to:

Explain the usefulness of long-term charting.

Review long-term charts critically and grasp the importance of their historical data.

READING ORIENTATION

Chapter 8 discusses the importance of long-term charts for analysis and forecasting purposes. Examples of weekly and monthly charts are plentiful. These charts also provide the reader with a review of concepts and price patterns covered in the previous chapters.

MIDTERM REVIEW

At the end of Lesson 6, you will have an opportunity to collectively assess your knowledge of the various topics and concepts introduced thus far. A quick review of the key terms in Lessons 1–6 will help you on the Midterm Assessment.

KEY TERMS

longer-range charts, 181–182

Perpetual Contract, 184

When you have completed the reading assignment for Lesson 6, proceed to the Midterm Examination, which includes questions covering Lesson 6 material.

MIDTERM ASSESSMENT

MATCHING QUIZ

A. _____ **apex**
B. _____ **bar chart**
C. _____ **broadening formation**
D. _____ **commodity futures**
E. _____ **confirmation**
F. _____ **continuation patterns**
G. _____ **creation of first Dow Average**
H. _____ **descriptive statistics**
I. _____ **divergence**
J. _____ **flags and pennants**
K. _____ **fundamentalists**
L. _____ **head and shoulders**
M. _____ **key reversal day**
N. _____ **large hedgers**
O. _____ **lines**
P. _____ **long-term charts**
Q. _____ **measured move**
R. _____ **measuring techniques**
S. _____ **M.T.A.**
T. _____ **neckline**
U. _____ **OBV**
V. _____ **open interest**
W. _____ **Perpetual Contract™**
X. _____ **price filter**
Y. _____ **price gaps**
Z. _____ **price pattern**
AA. _____ **Random Walk Theory**
BB. _____ **resistance**

1. Cash position of different groups.
2. A key turning point identified after the fact.
3. Study of causes of market movement.
4. Direction of market movement.
5. Reaction lows or troughs.
6. Horizontal trading bands.
7. Part of a head and shoulders pattern.
8. July 3, 1884.
9. Market Technicians Association.
10. Measure trends in terms of rates of ascent or descent.
11. Requiring a trendline be broken by a predetermined price increment.
12. Both a price and time chart.
13. A sudden trend reversal with little forewarning.
14. A sudden turnaround on heavy volume at the bottom of a bear market.
15. Total number of outstanding contracts.
16. Seen in five-year average of open interest.
17. Sudden price rally with a notable decline in open interest.
18. Diverging trendlines that look like an expanding triangle.
19. An open space on a bar chart where no trading has taken place.
20. Over-extended "rubber band" effect.
21. To do nothing.
22. Total amount of trading for a particular market day.
23. General agreement of indicators.
24. Data presented in a graph format.
25. An intersection point at the right where two trendlines meet.
26. Selling pressure is stronger than buying pressure.
27. Help determine long-term major trend and price objectives.
28. Price movement is random and unpredictable.

Second column continued on next page.

CC.____ saucer

DD.____ seasonal tendency

EE.____ selling climax

FF.____ speedlines

GG.____ spike

HH.____ support

II.____ technicians

JJ.____ trend

KK.____ triangle

LL.____ volume

29. Market advances or declines are divided into two equal and parallel moves.
30. Usually reflects sideways price action.
31. A line or curving volume indicator.
32. Preceded by a sharp, almost straight line move.
33. A slow gradual change in a trend.
34. A major and common reversal pattern.
35. All are traded on margin.
36. Indicators fail to confirm one another.
37. Study effects of market movement.
38. Bad signals.
39. Aid in determining minimum price objectives.
40. A continuous futures price history.
41. Most successful group in calling market turns.
42. Formation on a price chart.
43. Requires a minimum of four reversal points.

FILL-INS

1. A reversal pattern that is characterized by a slow and gradual trend change is called a ________________.
2. All futures are traded on ________________, usually less than 10%.
3. Technical analysts believe that market action ________________ everything.
4. The simplest and best known volume line indicator is ________________.
5. ________________ and ________________ are preceded by almost a straight line move.
6. An abrupt trend reversal with little or no warning, followed by a quick move in the opposite direction is called a ________________ pattern.
7. ________________ charts are not meant for trading purposes.

8. Market action includes the following principal data sources: __________, ______________, ______________________.

9. The vertical axis on a bar chart represents the ________________ of the contract.

10. When interpreting open interest, rising open interest in an uptrend is considered ________________.

11. ____________ ____________ are parallel trendlines drawn over or under the price action.

12. ____________ and ____________ ____________ are reported a day late.

13. The direction of peaks and troughs constitute a ____________ ____________.

14. In a ________________ ________________, the trendlines diverge.

15. Reaction lows are called ____________ ____________.

16. A ________________ ________________ or coil is usually a ________________ pattern.

17. Only the total ________________ and ____________ ____________ numbers are used for forecasting purposes.

18. A(n) ______________ triangle is bullish and a(n) ______________ triangle is bearish.

19. A long-term ________________ chart is linked by a number of contracts.

20. The ________________ ________________ provides years of price history on a continuum, as an alternative to using nearby months.

21. The proper order in long-term chart analysis is to begin with the ____________ ____________ and work toward the ____________ ____________.

MULTIPLE CHOICE

Refer to the following figure to answer question 1:

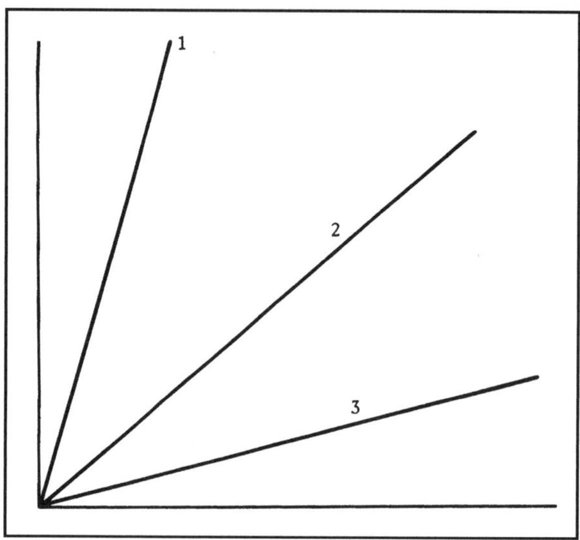

1. The most valid trendline is:
   a. line 1.
   b. line 2.
   c. lines 1 and 3.
   d. None of the above.

Refer to the following figure to answer question 2:

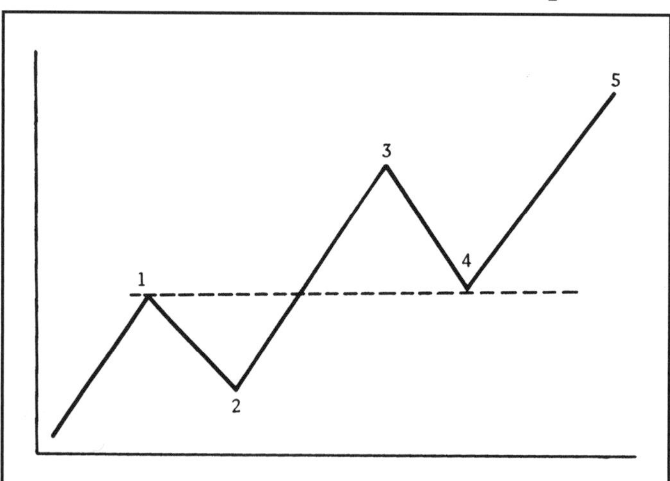

2. Points 1 and 4 are:
   a. Indicative of an uptrend.
   b. Resistance and support levels.
   c. Resistance levels only.
   d. A sideways pattern.

3. The technical analysis approach is based on:
   a. Market action discounting everything.
   b. Prices moving in trends.
   c. History repeating itself.
   d. All of the above.

4. In a valid double top:
   a. There are two distinguishable peaks at very different price levels.
   b. Volume is lighter on the first peak.
   c. Sometimes several bounces occur.
   d. Height is often used as a measuring technique.

Refer to the following figure to answer question 5:

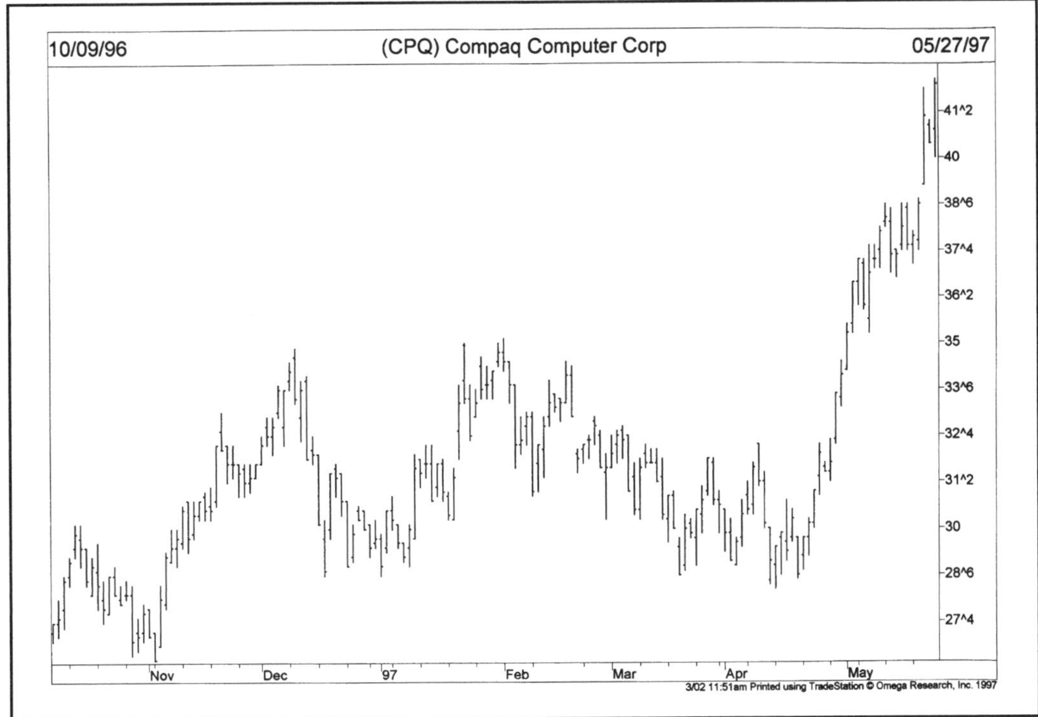

5. This is an example of a:
   a. Monthly continuation chart.
   b. Weekly continuation chart.
   c. Point and figure chart.
   d. A daily bar chart.

Refer to the following figure to answer question 6:

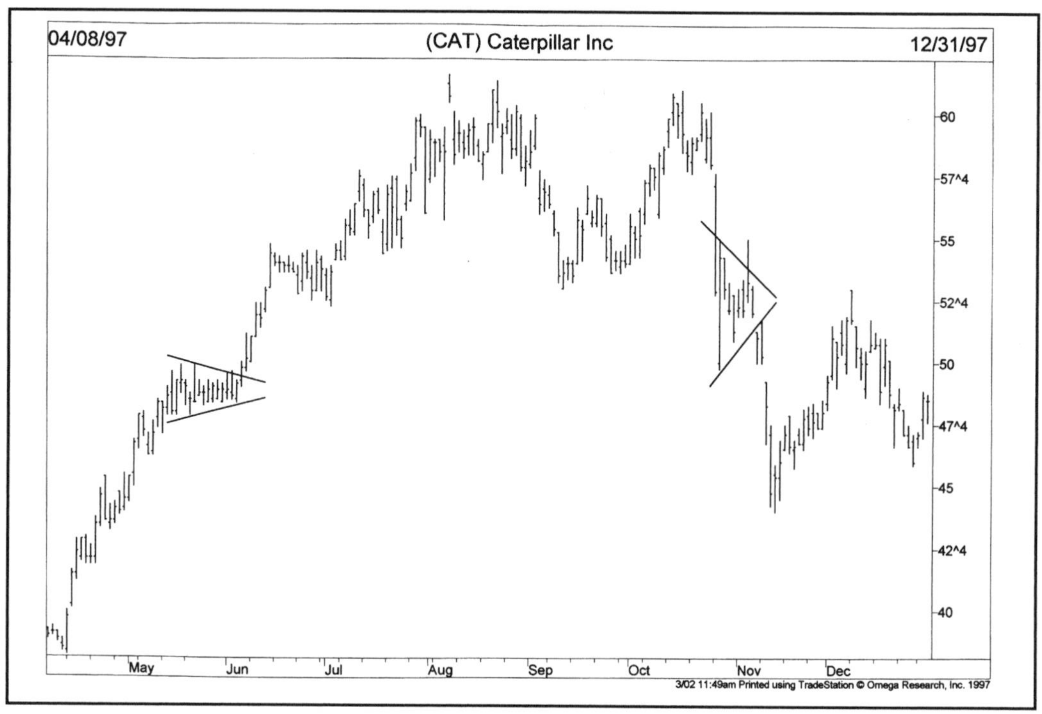

6. The two pairs of converging trendlines indicate:
   a. Pennants that continue the trend.
   b. Pennants that run counter to the trend.
   c. Flags that continue the trend.
   d. Flags that run counter to the trend.

Refer to the following figure to answer question 7:

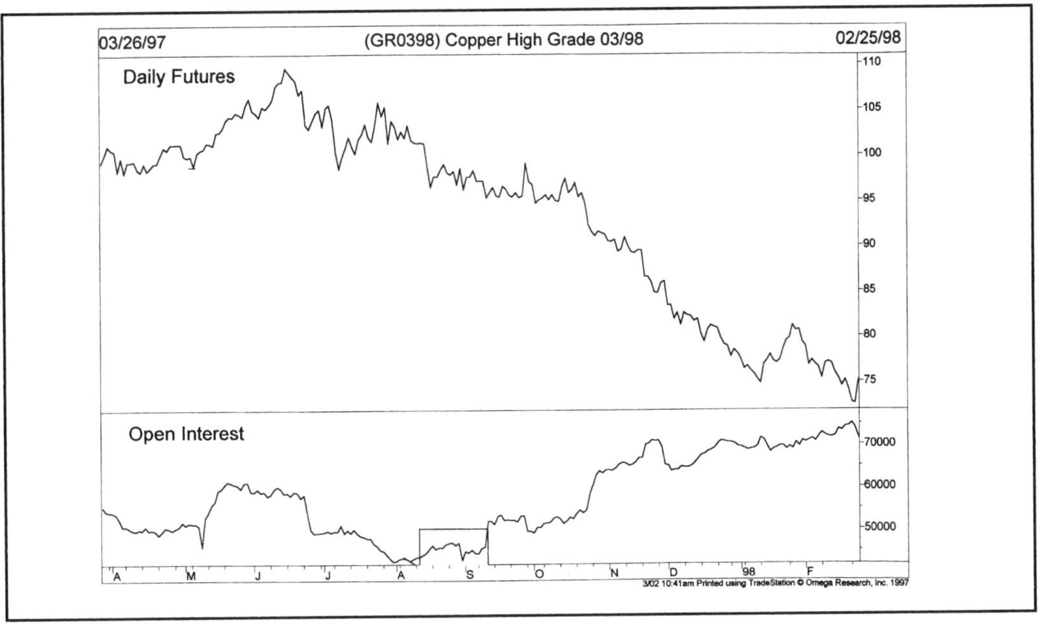

7. In this depiction:
   a. Open interest is giving off false signals.
   b. Declining open interest in the fall of 1997 is bullish.
   c. Rising open interest during the fall of 1997 confirms falling prices.
   d. Volume is light.

Refer to the following figure to answer question 8:

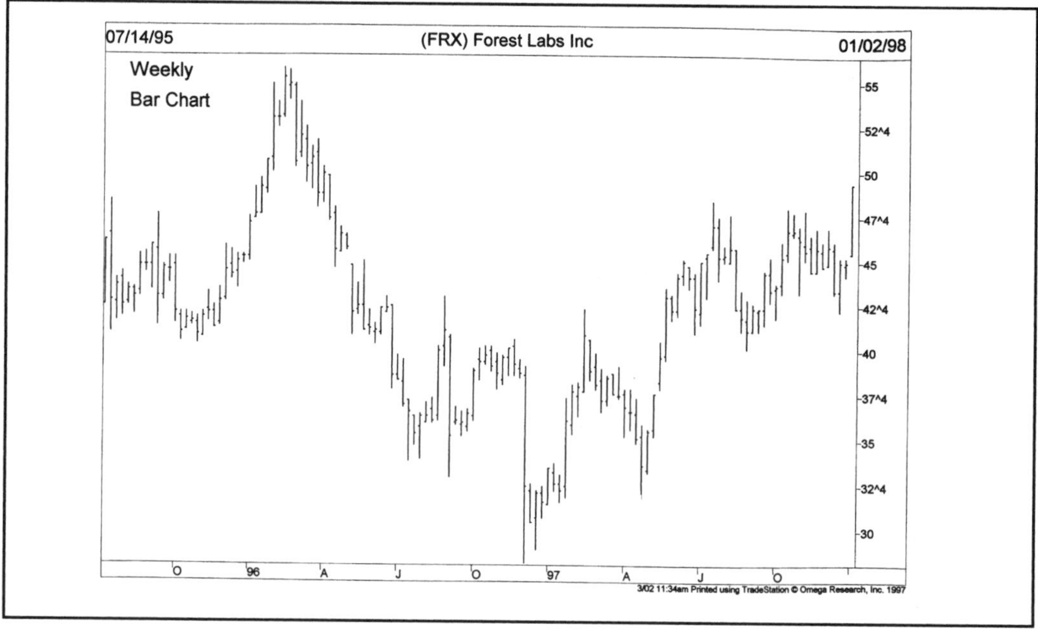

8. This is an example of:
   a. A triple top.
   b. A double head and shoulders bottom.
   c. A diamond.
   d. None of the above.

9. The Random Walk Theorists claim that:
   a. Price changes are "serially independent."
   b. Price changes are predictable.
   c. Buy and hold strategies are useless.
   d. None of the above.

10. According to Dow, market trends have:
    a. Six categories.
    b. Five categories.
    c. Two categories.
    d. Three categories.

11. Which most accurately describes a danger signal in a bull market at market tops?

a. An unusually high open interest.

b. Rising open interest in an uptrend.

c. Prices remaining in an uptrend.

d. All longs having winning positions.

Refer to the following figure to answer question 12:

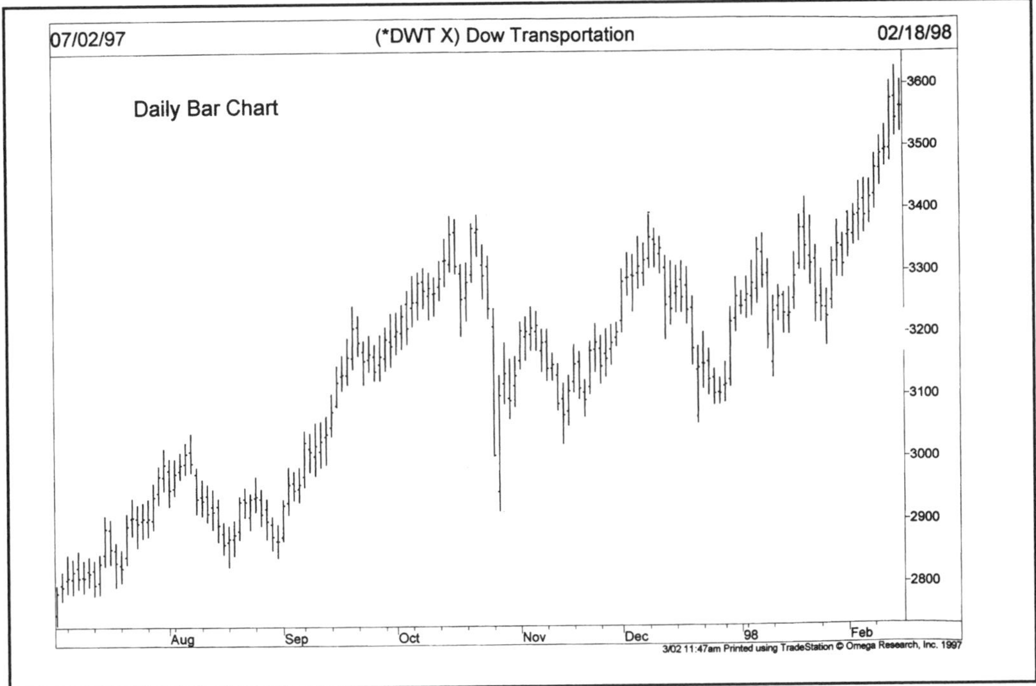

12. This figure represents:

a. Rising open interest.

b. A saucer.

c. An ascending triangle.

d. A nonpattern.

13. To confirm a trend, volume should:
   a. Reflect an island reversal pattern.
   b. Expand in the direction of the major trend.
   c. Reverse in the direction of the major trend.
   d. Move horizontally in the direction of the major trend.

Refer to the following figure to answer question 14:

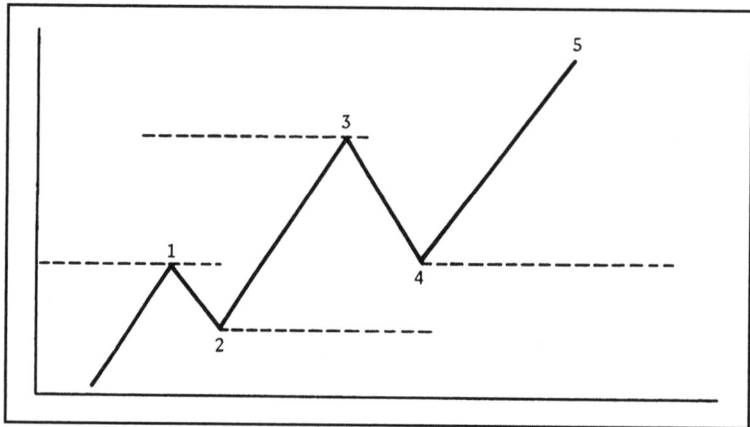

14. Points 1 and 3 are:
   a. Troughs.
   b. Support levels.
   c. Reaction lows.
   d. Resistance levels.

Refer to the following figure to answer question 15:

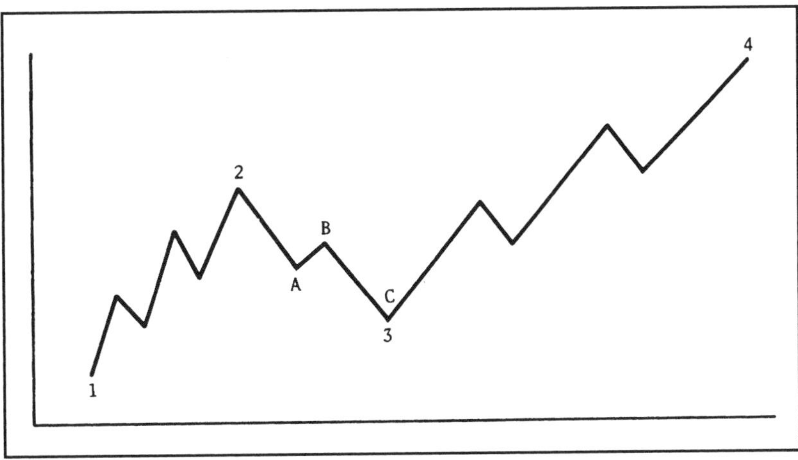

15. Points 1, 2, 3, and 4 show the:
    a. Secondary downtrend.
    b. Major uptrend.
    c. Minor uptrend.
    d. Secondary uptrend.

16. Which is not an example of a continuation pattern?
    a. Triangle.
    b. Rectangle.
    c. Pennant.
    d. Right angle.

17. Which is not true during a selling climax?
    a. Prices rise sharply first.
    b. There is heavy trading.
    c. There is a large decline in open interest.
    d. Prices drop sharply first.

Refer to the following figure to answer question 18:

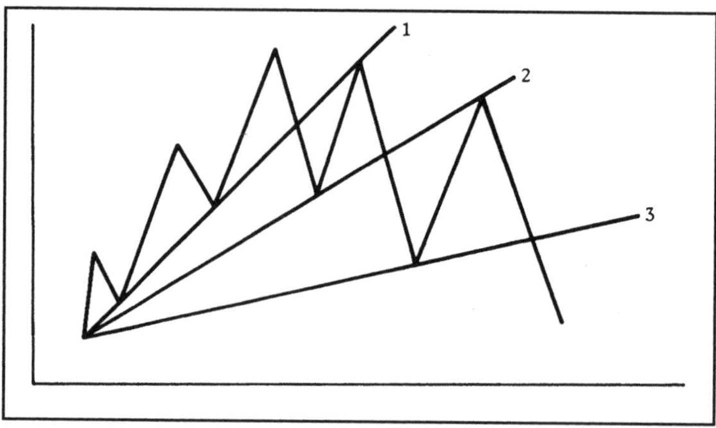

18. This figure depicts the:

a. Fan principle.

b. Signal of a trend reversal at point 3.

c. Trendlines at 1 and 2 becoming resistance lines.

d. All of the above.

Refer to the following figure to answer question 19:

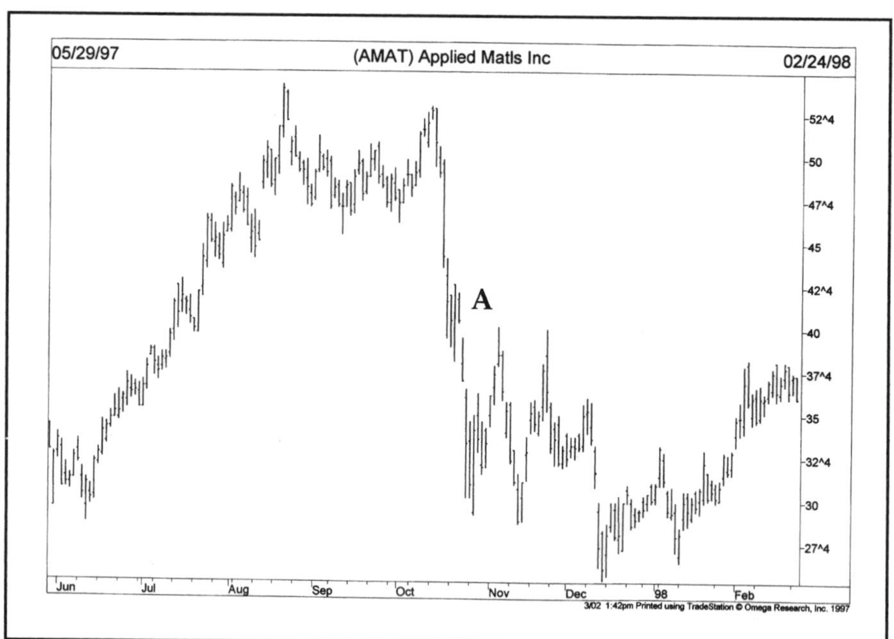

19. Point A reflects a(n):
    a. Exhaustion gap.
    b. Measuring gap.
    c. Retracement gap.
    d. Breakaway gap.

Refer to the following figure to answer question 20:

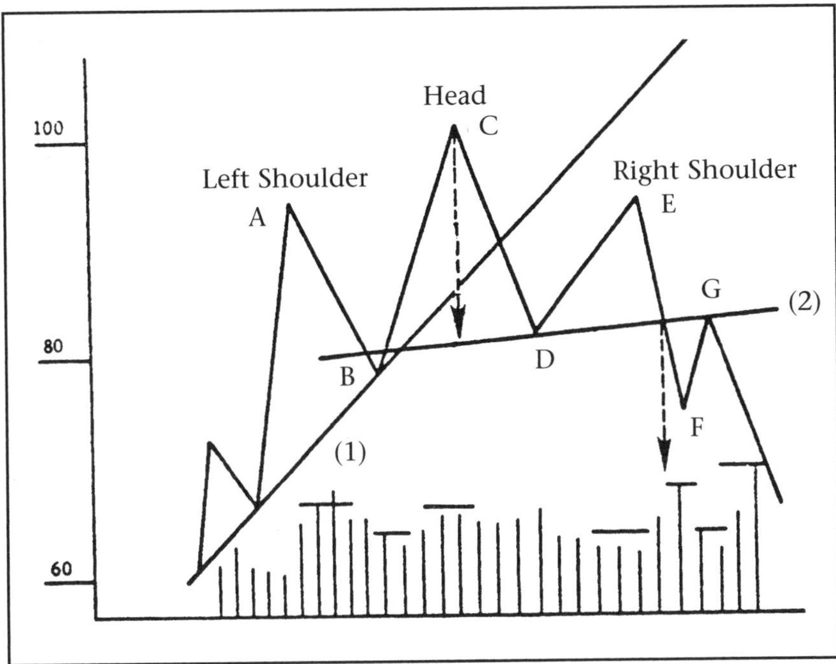

20. The line that forms along B, D, and G is the:
    a. Hairline.
    b. Neckline.
    c. Defensive posture line.
    d. Downward trendline.

Refer to the following figure to answer question 21:

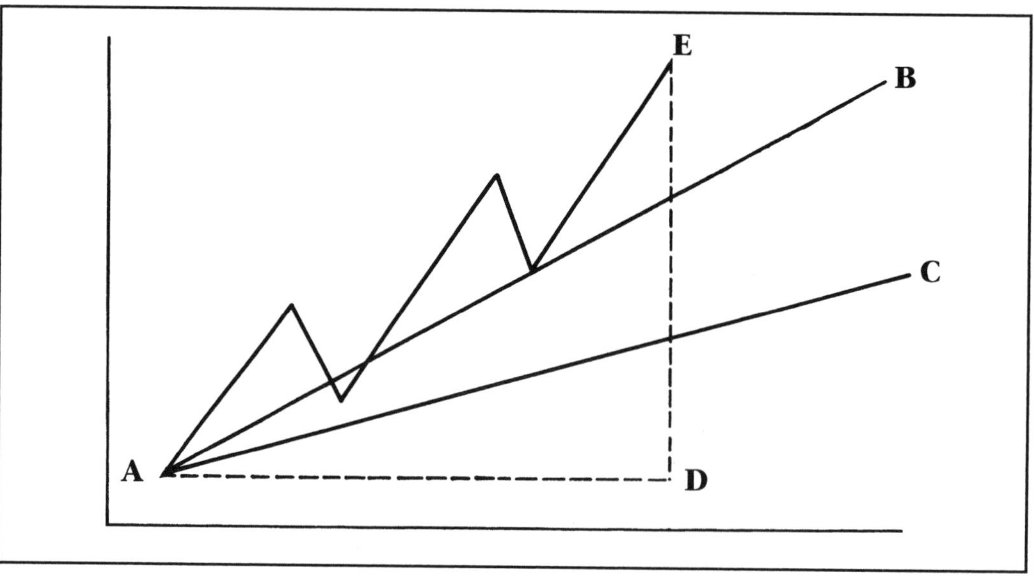

21. In this figure the 2/3 speedline is line:
    a. AB
    b. AC
    c. AD
    d. DE

22. The following is not common to all reversal patterns:
    a. The existence of a prior trend.
    b. The smaller the pattern, the greater the subsequent move.
    c. Bottoms usually take longer to build.
    d. All of the above.

Refer to the following figure to answer question 23:

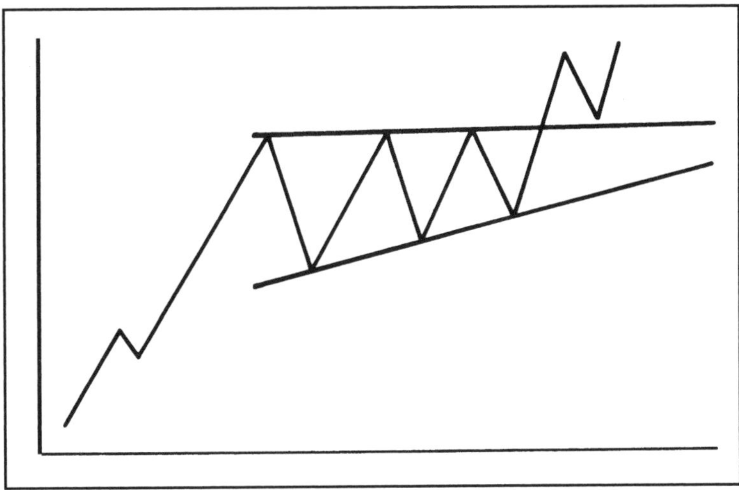

23. The figure represents a:
    a. Bullish descending triangle.
    b. Bearish descending triangle.
    c. Bullish ascending triangle.
    d. Bearish ascending triangle.

Refer to the following figure to answer question 24:

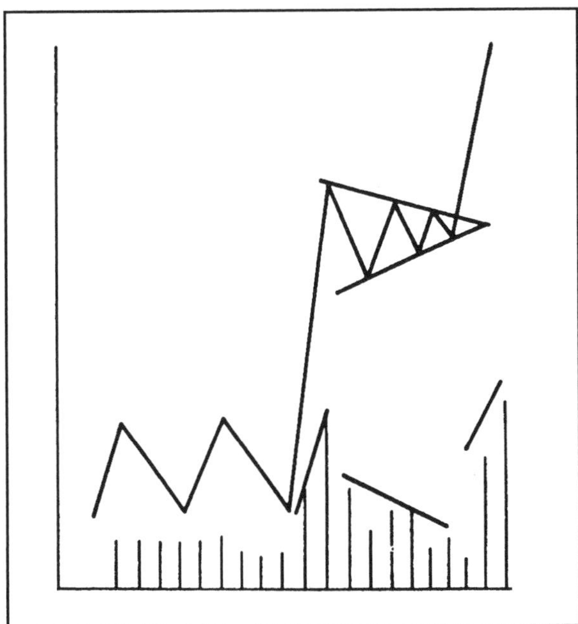

24. This is an example of a:
 a. Bullish pennant.
 b. Bullish flag.
 c. Bearish pennant.
 d. Bearish flag.

Refer to the following figure to answer question 25:

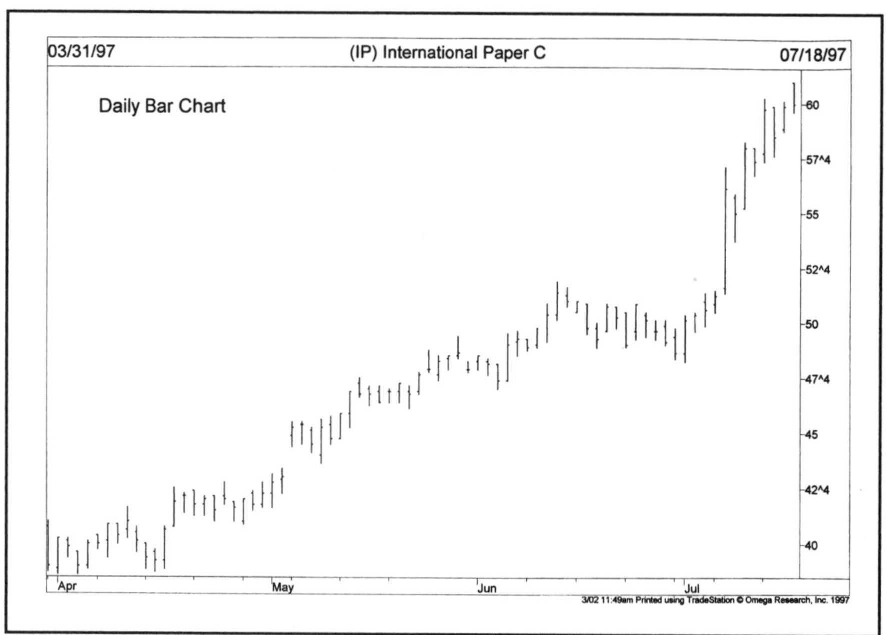

25. This figure contains a:
 a. Bullish pennant.
 b. Bearish pennant.
 c. Bullish flag.
 d. Bearish flag.

MIDTERM ANSWER SHEET

MATCHING QUIZ

A. 25	N. 41	AA. 28
B. 12	O. 6	BB. 26
C. 18	P. 27	CC. 33
D. 35	Q. 29	DD. 16
E. 23	R. 39	EE. 14
F. 30	S. 9	FF. 10
G. 8	T. 7	GG. 13
H. 24	U. 31	HH. 5
I. 36	V. 15	II. 37
J. 32	W. 40	JJ. 4
K. 3	X. 11	KK. 42
L. 34	Y. 19	LL. 22
M. 2	Z. 42	

FILL-INS

1. saucer
2. margin
3. discounts
4. OBV (on balance volume)
5. Flags ... pennants
6. V or spike
7. Long-term
8. price, volume, open interest
9. price
10. bullish
11. Channel lines
12. Volume ... open interest
13. market trend
14. Broadening formation
15. support levels
16. symmetrical triangle ... continuation
17. volume ... open interest
18. ascending ... descending
19. continuation
20. Perpetual Contract ™
21. long range ... near term

MULTIPLE CHOICE

1. **b** This is Figure 4.12 (on page 77). Line 2, which closely approximates a 45-degree angle, is the most valid trendline.
2. **b** See Figure 4.5a on page 62.
3. **d** All correctly state the basic premises of the technical approach. See page 1.
4. **d** There are two distinguishable peaks but they usually have similar price patterns. Volume tends to be heavy on the first peak, lighter on the second. Several return moves would not be reflective of a valid double top. See Figure 5.5a on page 118.
5. **d** This is Figure 6.9c, page 149. Each bar presents one day. Did you see the rectangular pattern?

6. a See Figure 6.7b on page 145. The first pennant continues the uptrend; the second continues the downtrend.
7. c In this figure (Figure 7.11, page 172), open interest clearly confirmed the price downtrend. Volume cannot be determined from this chart.
8. d This figure represents a head and shoulders bottom. Notice the slope of the neckline. There are no diamond patterns in this figure. See Figure 5.2b on page 111.
9. a Random Walk Theory states that prices are unpredictable, and the simplest strategy to follow is to buy and hold. See page 19-20.
10. d Dow identified three categories—the primary, secondary, and minor. Bear in mind that the number three shows up quite frequently in the technical analysis approach. For example, three sources of information—price, volume, and open interest. See page 26.
11. a A high open interest figure at market tops may even be a bearish signal, especially if the price drop is sudden. See page 172.
12. c This is Figure 6.3b on page 137. Open interest is not plotted on this figure. Nor does this figure reflect a saucer or nonpattern.
13. b Most horizontal trends reflect a pause in the market prior to the next upward or downward move. An island reversal pattern in isolation should not be used to predict a major trend move. See pages 163–164.
14. d See page 62, Figure 4.5a. Points 1 and 3 are resistance levels. Points 2 and 4 are support levels.
15. b These points reflect a major uptrend. A, B, and C are minor waves between points 2 and 3 which in and of themselves represent a secondary correction within the uptrend (Figure 4.2a, page 53).
16. d There is no such thing as a right angle continuation pattern.
17. a Prices drop sharply first. During "blowoffs," prices rise sharply first. B and C are also statements that apply to "selling climaxes." See pages 91-93, 175.
18. d This is an example of the fan principle (page 74-76). Note that trendlines 1 and 2 have become resistance lines, and point 3 signals the trend reversal.
19. b The bottom and top boxes enclose exhaustion gaps (Figure 4.23b, page 96).
20. b This is an example of a head and shoulders top. A and E are the shoulders, C is the head, and lines B, D, and G form the neckline. See Figure 5.1a, page 104.
21. a Developed by Edson Gould, speedlines divide the trend into thirds. They measure the rate of ascent or descent of a trend. See Figure 4.21a, page 88.
22. b Common to all reversal trends is a need for a prior trend, breaking of trendlines, top and bottom patterns—of which bottoms take longer to build; and the larger the price pattern the greater the subsequent move. See page 101-103.
23. c This is an example of a continuation pattern that is bullish. Note the rising lower line (Figure 6.1b, page 131). A bearish pattern would be reflective of a descending triangle.
24. a The bullish pennant resembles a small symmetrical triangle. Pennants and flags represent a brief pause in an otherwise dynamic market. See Figure 6.6b, on page 143.
25. c This is essentially the same pattern as in question 24. See Figure 6.7a, page 144.

LESSON SEVEN

Moving Averages

READING ASSIGNMENT

Chapter 9 of the text.

OBJECTIVES

After completing this lesson, you should be able to:

Realize the importance of this technical indicator.

Identify the three different types of moving averages.

Understand how moving averages are used.

Understand the concept of the weekly rule technique.

READING ORIENTATION

As you explore this chapter, you will see that moving averages are widely used and very informative as a trend-following system. As an indicator, they are precise and computer-programmable. A well-rounded background in this area will prove beneficial to the exacting technician.

KEY TERMS

arithmetic mean (simple moving average), 197, 199
Bollinger Bands, 209-211, 221
centering, 211
closing price, 197-198
double crossover method, 203-204
Fibonacci numbers, 212-213
four-week rule, 212, 215-219
harmonics, 218
linearly weighted moving average, 197, 199
moving average, 195-215
percentage envelopes, 207-208
standard deviation, 209
time cycles, 212
triple crossover method, 204

CHALLENGE

MATCHING QUIZ

A. __7__ arithmetic mean

B. _____ Bollinger Bands

C. _____ center

D. _____ closing price

E. _____ double crossover method

F. _____ 5, 10, 20, 40

G. _____ harmonics

H. _____ lead time

I. _____ linearly weighted moving average

J. _____ moving average

K. _____ percentage envelope

L. _____ 13, 21, 34, 55

M. _____ time cycles

N. _____ triple crossover method

1. 4-9-18 day moving average combination.
2. Two trading bands placed around a moving average.
3. A simple breakout system based on the monthly major cycle.
4. Average of a body of data.
5. A statistically correct way to plot a moving average.
6. Total divided by the sum of the multipliers.
7. Simple moving average.
8. Repetitive, measurable events that play a role in market movement.
9. Days often used for moving averages.
10. Price most often used for moving average analysis.
11. Signal to buy when the short crosses above the long average.
12. Parallel lines above and below the moving average line.
13. Each cycle is related to the next larger/shorter cycle by two.
14. Fibonacci series.
15. The moving average is placed days ahead of the actual price data.
16. The mean.

FILL-INS

1. The __________________ __________________ is used primarily as a trend-following device.

2. __________________ __________________ averages tend to be less sensitive to price action.

3. This type of indicator gives equal weight to each day's price: __________________________.

4. The ________________ moving average is most often used when prices are in nontrending periods.

5. When employing two moving averages the ________________ one is used for timing and the ________________ one for identifying a trend.

6. In the triple crossover system the 4-day average will follow the trend most closely, followed by the 9-day and then the ______-day.

7. One of the best known commodity market cycles is the ________________ cycle.

8. Moving averages work best as indicators when the market is in a ________________ period.

9. This breakout system is based on the dominant monthly cycle: ________________.

MULTIPLE CHOICE

1. Short-term moving averages:
   - **a.** Work better in sideways patterns.
   - **b.** Generate more frequent false signals.
   - **c.** Are precise.
   - **d.** All of the above.

2. Which is one of the best known time cycles?
   - **a.** Bimonthly cycle.
   - **b.** 15-day cycle.
   - **c.** Harmonic cycle.
   - **d.** Monthly cycle.

3. Which statement is most accurate when closing prices move above the moving average?
   a. A buy signal is recommended.
   b. A hold signal is recommended.
   c. A sell signal is recommended.
   d. A sideways pattern will develop next.

4. The moving average is:
   a. Not a technical indicator.
   b. Subjective.
   c. A trend-following system.
   d. Largely ignored by technicians.

Refer to the following figure to answer question 5:

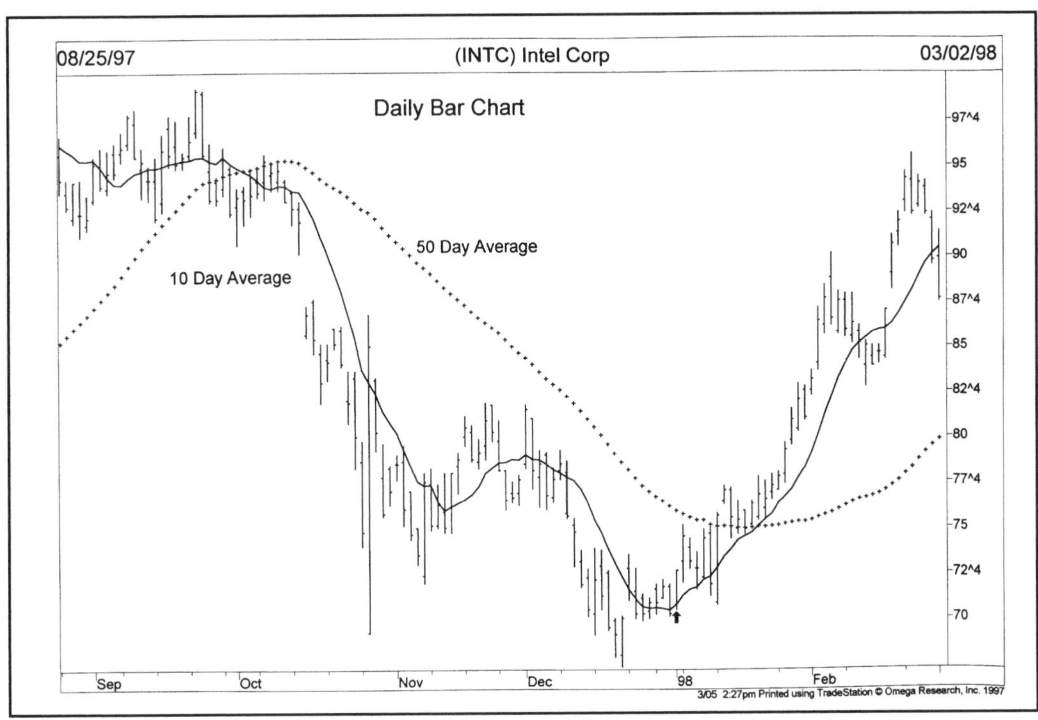

5. Compared with the longer moving average, the 10-day moving average:
   a. Is slower.
   b. Is more reliable.
   c. Gives an earlier signal of the upturn.
   d. Gives a timely sell signal in February.

6. When using Bollinger Bands:
   a. The simplest approach is to use the upper and lower bands as targets.
   b. The bands always stay a constant percentage apart.
   c. When the bands diverge, look for a new trend.
   d. When the bands converge, look for the trend to continue.

7. The linearly weighted moving average attempts to:
   a. Smooth out the moving average.
   b. Correct the weighting problem.
   c. Discount price action.
   d. Diminishes the weight given the most recent closing day.

8. What do cyclic analysts use most often to isolate underlying markets?
   a. The centering technique.
   b. The triple crossover method.
   c. Lead time.
   d. The reverse tally outcome system.

9. The most common application of the moving average is to:
   a. The last 10 days' prices.
   b. The last month's prices.
   c. The last quarter's prices.
   d. The last year's prices.

10. The exponentially smoothed moving average:
    a. Assigns a lesser weight to recent price action.
    b. Lacks sophistication.
    c. Discounts price data.
    d. Includes the entire price data of a specific futures contract.

11. Percentage "envelopes" can be used to:
    a. Determine when a market is overextended.
    b. Estimate volume.
    c. Estimate open interest.
    d. None of the above.

12. The system using the four preceding calendar weeks rule states:
    a. Cover long positions when prices fall.
    b. Liquidate long positions and sell short positions when prices fall.
    c. Liquidate short positions and cover long positions when prices rise.
    d. Cover short positions and liquidate long positions when prices rise.

Refer to the following figure to answer question 13:

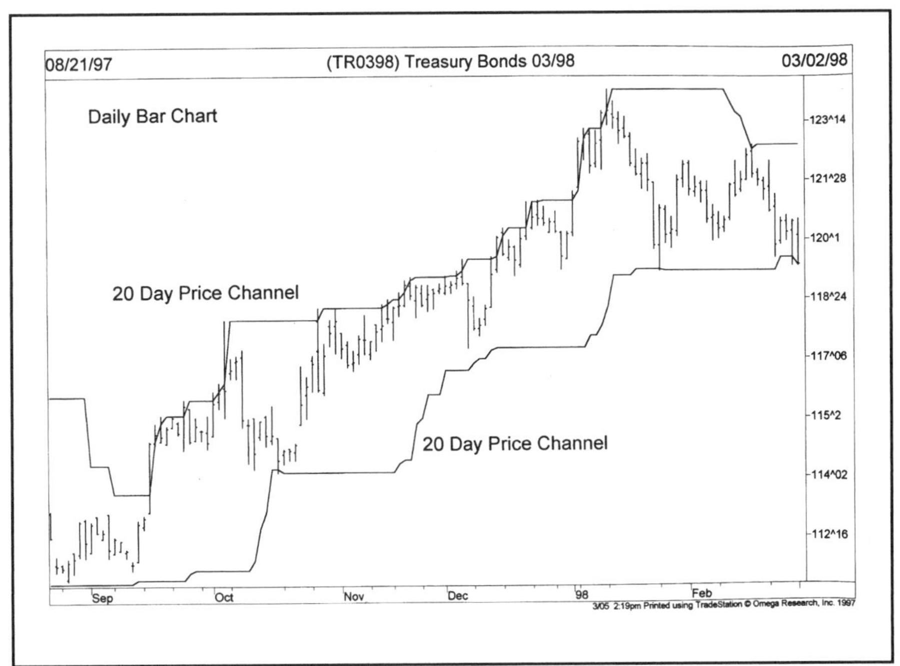

13. In relation to the upper 20-day channel, prices are signaling:
    a. Sell.
    b. Buy.
    c. Wait and see.
    d. Sell short.

14. Another trend-following technique besides the moving average is:
    a. Weekly price channel.
    b. Rounding price channel.
    c. Line price channel.
    d. Exponential price channel.

15. Which statement(s) is/are true?
    a. Moving averages are trend predictors.
    b. Moving averages perform poorly in sideways markets.
    c. Moving averages are rarely used by technicians.
    d. None of the above.

16. In the triple crossover system, which statement is most true?
    a. 4-11-28 is a popular combination.
    b. A buy alert occurs in an uptrend when day 4 crosses days 11 and 18.
    c. The 4-day average follows the trend the closest.
    d. All of the above.

17. When two moving averages are used:
    a. A buy signal results from the shorter average moving below the larger one.
    b. A sell signal results from the shorter average moving above the longer one.
    c. The two averages lead the market.
    d. The number of whipsaws is reduced.

Refer to the following figure to answer question 18:

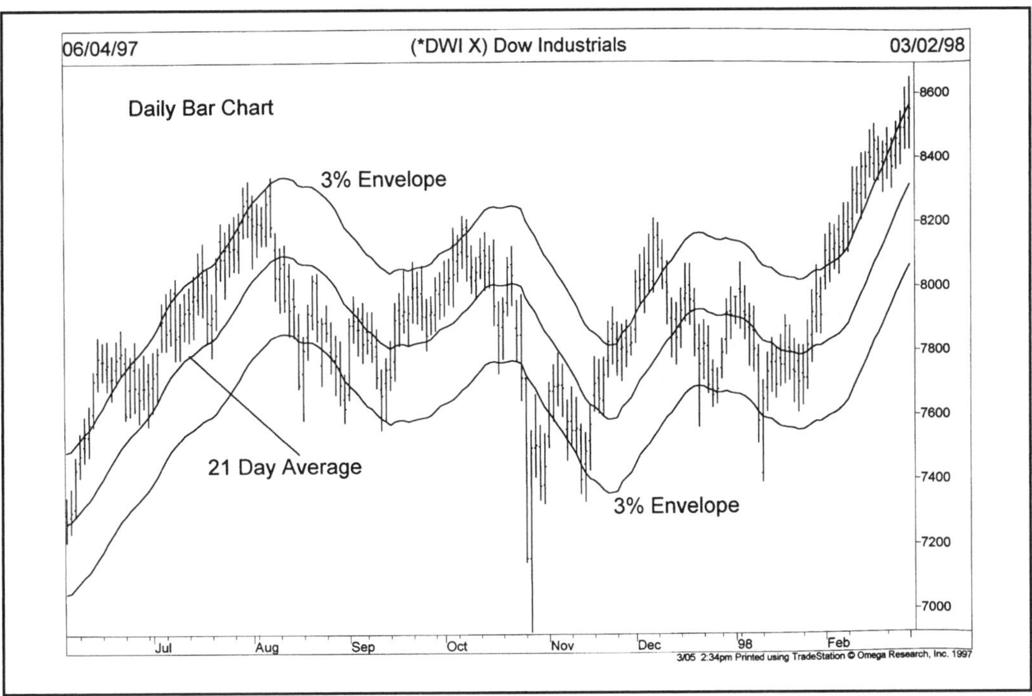

18. This is an example of:
 a. The use of filters.
 b. The use of envelopes.
 c. The use of Fibonacci numbers.
 d. All of the above.

19. The simple moving average:
 a. Covers an extensive trading period.
 b. Weights recent prices more than distant ones.
 c. Is used by most technical analysts.
 d. Is also known as the linearly weighted moving average.

ANSWER SHEET

MATCHING QUIZ

A. 7
B. 2
C. 5
D. 10
E. 11
F. 9
G. 13
H. 15
I. 6
J. 4
K. 12
L. 14
M. 8
N. 1

FILL-INS

1. moving average
2. Long-range
3. simple moving average
4. short-term
5. shorter ... longer
6. 18-
7. monthly
8. trending
9. The four-week rule

MULTIPLE CHOICE

1. **d** As the answer implies, short-term moving averages work best in sideways patterns. Although they are more sensitive indicators than long moving averages, they also tend to give off more frequent false signals. Moving averages are not subjective but give precise signals. See page 197.
2. **d** The best known cycle is the monthly cycle. Harmonic is a principle in cyclic analysis where each cycle is related to a shorter/longer cycle by two. See page 212.
3. **a** As prices move above the moving average, a buy signal is advised. A sell signal is recommended when prices move below the moving average. There is no evidence to suggest that a sideways pattern will develop as a result of price moving above or below the moving average. See Figure 9.12, page 220.
4. **c** The moving average is a trend-following technical indicator that is quite precise and widely used by technicians. See pages 197.
5. **c** Shorter averages are faster, less reliable, and can give premature signals. See Figure 9.4, page 202.
6. **a** Bollinger Bands tend to expand and contract with the last 20 days' volatility. Diverging bands can signal the end of a trend; converging bands, a continuation. See page 210-211.
7. **b** The linearly weighted moving average is designed to correct the weighting problem. The smoothed average occurs when using the exponentially smoothing average technique. The linearly weighted approach gives greater weight to the more recent closing days. See page 199.

8. a Centering is the statistically correct method for plotting averages and is preferred by cyclic analysts. The triple crossover method employs three different days of moving averages. Although lead time is used in placing averages, it is not the preferred method by cyclic analysts. See page 211.

9. a Moving averages are most commonly applied to daily bar charts, although they certainly could be used with long-term charts. See page 195.

10. d The exponentially moving average does not discount price action. It is an exact technique—quite sophisticated—and assigns greater weight to the more recent action. See pages 199–200.

11. a Envelopes have nothing to do with volume or open interest. See page 207-208.

12. b The basic premise behind the four-week rule is to liquidate long position and sell short position when prices fall. Conversely, cover short positions and buy long when prices exceed the highs of the previous four calendar weeks. See pages 212, 215-219.

13. b The buy signal comes in late September. See Figure 9.11, page 219.

14. a Aside from moving averages, the weekly price channel or weekly rule, as it is commonly known, is another trend-following technique. See page 215.

15. b Moving averages are trend-following; they are not market predictors of future trends. Moving averages are used frequently by technicians. Moving averages work best when markets are trending, and perform poorly in sideways markets. See page 196-197.

16. c 4-11-28 is not a popular average. Since these combinations are not part of the triple crossover method, a buy alert does not occur when day four crosses days 11 and 28. The four-day average follows the trend most closely and would signal a buy alert if it crossed over days 9 and 18. See page 204.

17. d All of the first three statements are false. See page 203.

18. d This figure shows how 3% envelopes are used with 21-day moving averages. Envelopes are filters. See Figure 9.8a, page 208.

19. c The simple moving average covers only a 10-day period and weights each day equally. It is also known as the arithmetic mean. See page 199.

LESSON EIGHT

Oscillators and Contrary Opinion

READING ASSIGNMENT

Chapter 10 of the text.

OBJECTIVES

After completing this lesson, you should be able to:

- Explain how oscillators are used.
- Identify divergences.
- Apply the Contrary Opinion method.
- Identify the characteristics of overbought and oversold market conditions.

READING ORIENTATION

This chapter is primarily about oscillators and how this technique is employed by technicians to determine overbought and oversold market conditions. The use of oscillators is another important technique available to the technicians that further enhances their ability to respond to market trends.

KEY TERMS

Bullish consensus numbers, 258-260
Commodity Channel Index, 237-239
Contrary Opinion, 226, 257-261
danger zones, 245
divergence, 227
failure swings, 242
K%D, 246-248
MACD, 252-255
momentum, 228-233
oscillator, 226-228
%R, 249-250
rate of change (ROC), 234
Relative Strength Index (RSI), 239-245
zero line, 189, 230-231

CHALLENGE

MATCHING QUIZ

A. __4__ bullish consensus numbers
B. _____ Contrary Opinion
C. _____ danger zones
D. _____ divergence
E. _____ failure swings
F. _____ K%D
G. _____ MACD
H. _____ momentum
I. _____ oscillator
J. _____ %R
K. _____ ROC
L. _____ relative strength index (RSI)
M. _____ zero line

1. The opposite of majority agreement.
2. Oscillator and price line move in opposite directions.
3. Left/right conversion symbols.
4. A weekly indicator of market sentiment.
5. Vertical scale from 0 to 100.
6. The Stochastic Process.
7. Crossing of line generates buy and sell signals.
8. Aids in identifying overbought and oversold conditions.
9. Reading above 20 is overbought, below 80 is oversold.
10. Identification of boundary extremes.
11. Measures the velocity of prices.
12. Warn of extremely overbought or oversold conditions.
13. The RSI is above 70 or below 30 before reversing.
14. An oscillator using two exponential moving averages.
15. The line falls within a +1 or –1 range.
16. Rate of change.

FILL-INS

1. In conjunction with price charts, ____________________ can identify short-term market extremes.
2. As a rule, crossing the ______________________________ usually signals important trading signals.
3. The measurement of ____________________ requires the taking of price differences for a fixed time interval.
4. The momentum indicator measures the rate of __________________ or __________________.
5. The RSI uses a vertical scale when movement above __________ is overbought and a move below __________ is oversold.

6. When a double top or bottom is formed on an oscillator, possible ________________ exists.

7. Two lines are used in the stochastic process–__________ line and the __________ line.

8. Using price ratios is one method to measure the __________ __________ __________ __________.

9. ________________ ________________ assesses the degree of bullishness or bearishness among speculators.

10. If the Bullish Consensus numbers are above 75%, a __________ might be near.

11. Oscillators are especially valuable toward the __________ of market moves.

12. The ________________ ________________ leads the advance or decline of the price movement by a few days.

MULTIPLE CHOICE

Please refer to the following figure to answer questions 1–3:

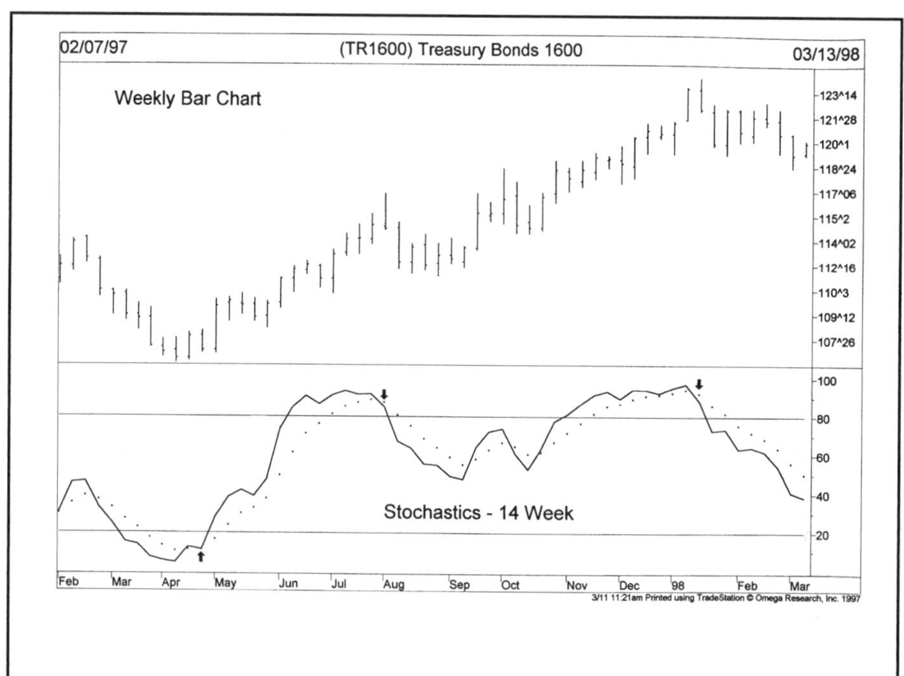

1. The solid curve at the bottom of the figure represents:
   a. %K.
   b. ROC.
   c. %D.
   d. MACD.

2. The dotted curve at the bottom of the figure represents:
   a. %K.
   b. ROC.
   c. %D.
   d. MACD.

3. Sell signals occur in:
   a. April and October.
   b. August and January.
   c. September and October.
   d. June and July.

4. Oscillators are most useful when:
   a. Its value is at extreme boundaries.
   b. There is divergence.
   c. The zero line is crossed.
   d. All of the above.

5. Which statement is most accurate?
   a. Momentum charts lack a zero line.
   b. Crossing above the zero line is used as a trading signal.
   c. A cross above the zero line is a sell signal.
   d. A cross below the zero line is a buy signal.

6. When two moving averages are too far apart:
   a. A downtrend is likely.
   b. The trend will probably not stall.
   c. A market extreme is created.
   d. Oscillators will provide little new information.

7. The RSI resolves the problem of:
   a. Erratic movement caused by sharp price changes.
   b. Equalization.
   c. Needing upper and lower boundary ranges.
   d. All of the above.

Refer to the following figure to answer questions 8 and 9:

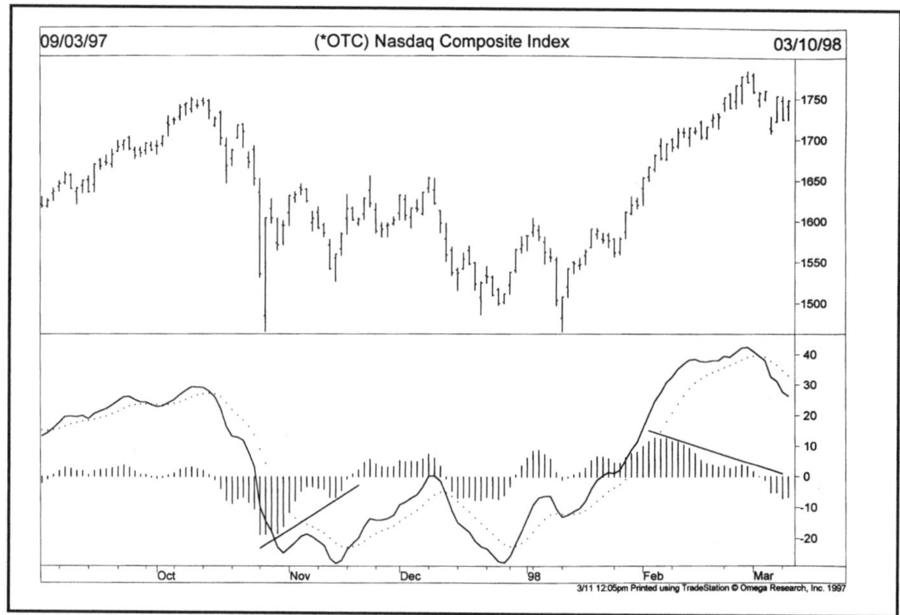

8. The vertical stripes at the bottom of the chart represent:
   a. The difference between opening and closing prices.
   b. The difference between two MACD lines.
   c. Volume.
   d. Open interest.

9. Trading signals occur in:
   a. October and November.
   b. November and December.
   c. February and March.
   d. None of the above.

10. In the stochastic process, the:
   a. %D line is of secondary importance to the %K line.
   b. %R line is a minor trend indicator.
   c. %K line is irrelevant.
   d. %D line is more important in signaling major trends.

11. The simplest way to use the oscillator is to:
   a. Use a binormal measuring system.
   b. Use stochastics.
   c. Measure the rate of change.
   d. Establish the zero line as a signal indicator.

12. The 70 and 30 lines are often used to:
   a. Form the %R oscillator.
   b. Establish the beginning of non-trending patterns.
   c. Generate signals.
   d. All of the above.

13. The most widely followed oscillator is the:
   a. ROC.
   b. RSI.
   c. MACD.
   d. K%D.

14. Which statement is the *most* accurate?
   a. Oscillators are good indicators to buy or sell right at a breakout.
   b. Oscillator interpretation can override basic trend analysis early in a breakout.
   c. Oscillators are better indicators later in a market move.
   d. Oscillators lose significance as a market movement matures.

15. Which statement is most accurate?
    a. Peaks and troughs on a price chart coincide with peaks and troughs on the oscillator in choppy markets.
    b. Oscillators are poor monitors of sideways price movement.
    c. Greater attention to oscillators is necessary in the early stages of a move.
    d. Oscillators tend to give off frequent false signals as the move reaches maturity.

16. A true contrarian:
    a. Has little use for the technical analysis approach.
    b. Follows the fundamental analyst's philosophy.
    c. Will act in the opposite direction of the majority.
    d. All of the above.

17. When two declining peaks are formed as prices continue to move higher, a bearish divergence occurs when the:
    a. K line is above 70.
    b. D line is above 70.
    c. D line is below 70.
    d. D line is below 30.

18. In Williams %R:
    a. An overbought reading is below 20.
    b. An oversold reading is above 80.
    c. A time period of one-third cycle length is used.
    d. None of the above.

19. In using ROC, if the latest price is higher than the price 10 days ago:
    a. The ratio would be between +1 and –1.
    b. The ratio would be above 100.
    c. The ratio would be below 100.

d. The ratio would hold at a constant until the market changed trends.

20. An important requirement for divergence analysis is that the:

a. Divergence must incorporate the principle of stochastics.

b. Divergence must be temporary.

c. Divergence occurs near oscillator extremes.

d. All of the above.

ANSWER SHEET

MATCHING QUIZ

A. 4
B. 1
C. 12
D. 2
E. 13
F. 6
G. 14
H. 11
I. 8
J. 9
K. 16
L. 5
M. 7

FILL-INS

1. oscillators
2. zero line
3. market momentum
4. ascent ... descent
5. 70 ... 30
6. divergence
7. %K line ... %D line
8. rate of change (ROC)
9. Contrary Opinion
10. top
11. end
12. momentum line

MULTIPLE CHOICE

1. **a** The curve is %K and the dashed line is %D. "ROC" stands for rate of change, and "MACD" stands for Moving Average Convergence/Divergence. See Figure 10.15, page 248.
2. **c** See the explanation for question 1.
3. **b** A sell signal occurs when the faster %K line crosses below the slower %D line. This occurs in August and January.
4. **d** Choices a, b, and c are the three most important uses for the oscillator. The described situations are common to most oscillators. See page 227.
5. **b** In its most simple form, the crossing of the zero line is used as a trading signal. Momentum charts have zero lines. Answers c and d are confusing in that a cross above the zero line is a buy signal, while a cross below is a sell signal. See pages 230.
6. **c** As the moving averages move farther apart, market extremes are created. Oscillators are important data sources. However, it is presumptuous to say that a downtrend will occur or that the trend will not stall. See page 227.
7. **d** The relative strength index (RSI) solves the problem of erratic movement caused by sharp price changes. Boundary lines are also part of the RSI. See page 232, 239-240.
8. **b** The vertical stripes make up a histogram, which represents the difference between two MACD lines. See Figure 10.20a, page 256.

9. a&b Zero line crossings generate trading signals. In Figure 10.20a, the histogram crosses before the MACD lines, giving traders some warning.

10. d In the stochastic process, the %D line is of primary importance and the %K line is secondary. The %R oscillator differs somewhat from the stochastic process. See pages 246-249.

11. d The simplest way to use oscillators is to establish the zero line as a signal indicator. Binominal systems are not relevant to oscillators. Stochastics are complicated, although quite useful. The rate of change is a ratio construct which again is useful though not necessarily simple. See pages 230-231.

12. c The 70/30 lines are used to generate buy/sell signals. They are not intended to establish nontrending patterns, since market conditions dictate such patterns.

13. b Technicians most often employ the RSI. Although the other techniques are also used, the RSI is the most widely followed. See page 239-240.

14. c Oscillators gain significance as a market move matures. See page 251-252.

15. a Choice a is the most accurate statement. Oscillators provide important information during sideways markets. Oscillators work best when the move has matured, not when it first begins. See page 251-252.

16. c A true contrarian acts in the opposite direction of the majority. Although they are grouped under the technical analysis approach, they tend to utilize a psychological analysis approach to market moves. See pages 257–258.

17. b Answer b is correct. When the D line is below 30, a bullish divergence is possible. See pages 246–247.

18. d In Williams %R, an overbought reading is above 20. An oversold reading is under 80. The time period is one-half the cycle length. See Figure 10.18, pages 250.

19. b "The ratio is above 100" is the correct response. +1 and –1 designations are not used in the ROC. Zero as a constant is not used in this system. See page 234.

20. c This is a basic point to remember about oscillators—divergence occurs near oscillator extremes. Stochastics and divergence are not interdependent on each other. "Divergence must be temporary" is not supported in the readings. See page 227.

LESSON NINE

Point and Figure Charting and Japanese Candlesticks

READING ASSIGNMENT

Chapters 11 and 12.

OBJECTIVES

After completing this lesson, you should be able to:

Read, plot, and explain the uses of point and figure charts.

Read, plot, and explain the uses of Japanese candlesticks.

READING ORIENTATION

These two chapters depart from the discussion of bar charts. Depending on the type of trading, a point and figure chart can be used as another valuable technical indicator. Samples are provided to help the reader develop a "feel" for plotting. It will quickly become obvious that this sample technique is easy to learn and can provide the technician with important trading information.

The Japanese candlestick chart, while used for centuries in Japan, is a relative newcomer for Western analysts. It is another important tool in market analysis.

KEY TERMS

black body, 298
body, 298
box size, 268-270
buy signal, 280–282, 286
catapult, 275
channel lines, 280-281
congestion area, 274
Dark Cloud Cover, 302, 311
Doji candlesticks, 300-301
Evening Star, 250, 303-304, 312
Falling Three Methods, 251, 304-305, 315
45-degree line, 282
fulcrum, 275
horizontal count, 274–275
horizontal measurement, 274-275, 286
intraday point and figure chart, 270-273
Long Day, 299
Morning Star, 303, 312
o column, 267
Piercing Line, 249, 302-303, 311
point and figure chart, 265-296
pole, 288
reversal candle patterns, 301-304
reversal criterion, 268-269
Rising Three Methods, 304-305, 315
sell signal, 280-281, 286
shadow (wick or hair), 298
Short Day, 299
Spinning Tops, 299-300
three-point reversal chart, 277-282
vertical measurement, 274-275, 286
Victor de Villiers, 265
white body, 298
x column, 267

CHALLENGE

MATCHING QUIZ

A. __20__ black body
B. _____ body
C. _____ box size
D. _____ catapult
E. _____ channel lines
F. _____ congestion area
G. _____ Dark Cloud Cover
H. _____ Doji candlesticks
I. _____ Evening Star
J. _____ fulcrum
K. _____ horizontal count
L. _____ intraday point and figure chart
M. _____ Long Days
N. _____ Morning Star
O. _____ o column
P. _____ Piercing Line
Q. _____ point and figure chart
R. _____ reversal candle pattern
S. _____ reversal criterion
T. _____ Rising Three Method
U. _____ sell signal
V. _____ shadow (wick/hair)
W. _____ Short Day
X. _____ white body
Y. _____ x column

1. Value assigned to each box on a chart.
2. Rectangle representing the difference between the day's open and close.
3. Shadows of varying lengths.
4. The width of the pattern.
5. Represents declining prices.
6. A retracement of boxes necessary to cause a reversal.
7. Study of pure price movement.
8. A column of o's decline one box below the lowest o in the prior column.
9. Used primarily as timing aids.
10. Three-day reversal pattern.
11. A congestion area that forms an accumulation base or distribution top.
12. Bullish reversal pattern.
13. A form of cash flow analysis.
14. Sideways price movement with well-defined tops/bottoms.
15. A breakout.
16. Widely used by floor traders.
17. Upper and lower shadows are longer than body.
18. Two-day bearish reversal.
19. Opening and closing prices are the same.
20. Close price was lower than open price.
21. Great difference between open and close prices.
22. For example, Dark Cloud Cover or Piercing Line.
23. Small difference between close and open prices.
24. Line above or below the body.
25. A candlestick construction pattern.
26. Represents rising prices.
27. Close price is higher than the open.

FILL-INS

1. The ____________ ____________ helps determine in advance the direction of the breakout.
2. The ____________ ____________ ____________ ____________ doesn't take time into consideration as the price action is plotted.
3. Trading signals are more/less precise on point and figure charts than on bar charts. ____________
4. Two candlestick reversal patterns are ____________ ____________ ____________ and ____________ ____________.
5. The two basic parts of a candlestick are the ____________ and the ____________.
6. If the closing price is higher than the opening price, the body of the candlestick is white/black. ____________
7. ____________ is not included on point and figure charts.
8. Point and figure charts provide the technician with specific ____________ and ____________ points.
9. The candlestick is a ____________ Day if the difference between the close and open prices is small.
10. A market condition where no three-box reversals occur during a trend is called a ____________.
11. The most important value of point and figure charts is the ability of the technician to identify ____________ and ____________ zones.
12. The ____________ ____________ ____________ ____________ ____________ technique is most useful for very short-term trading.
13. The lengths of the shadows vary in ____________ ____________.

MULTIPLE CHOICE

Refer to the following charts to answer questions 1 and 2:

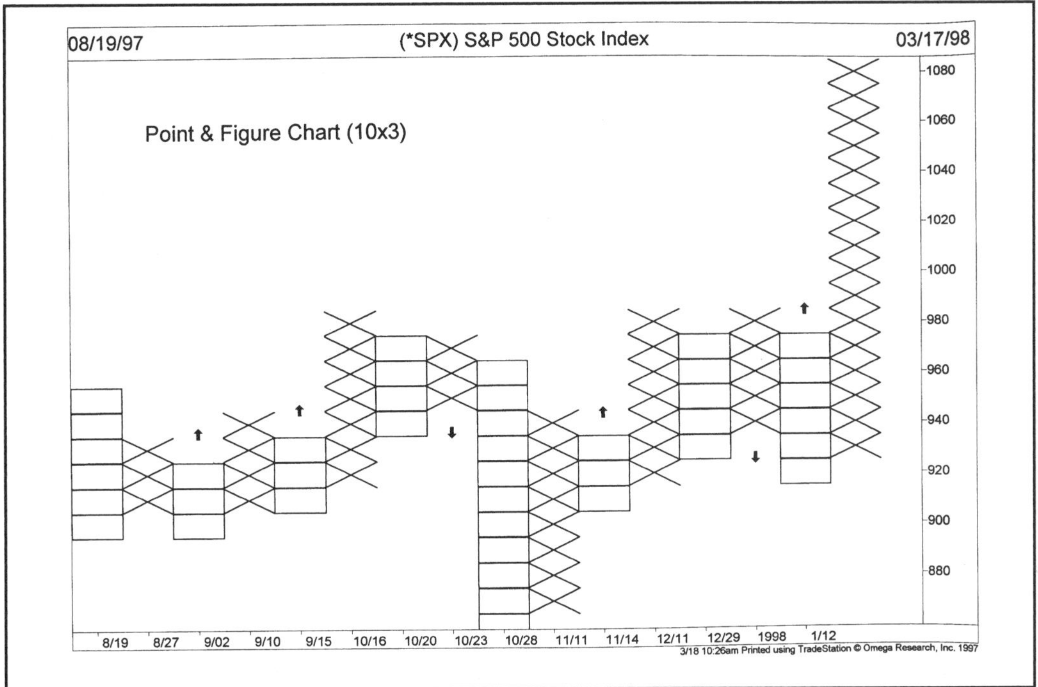

Figure A

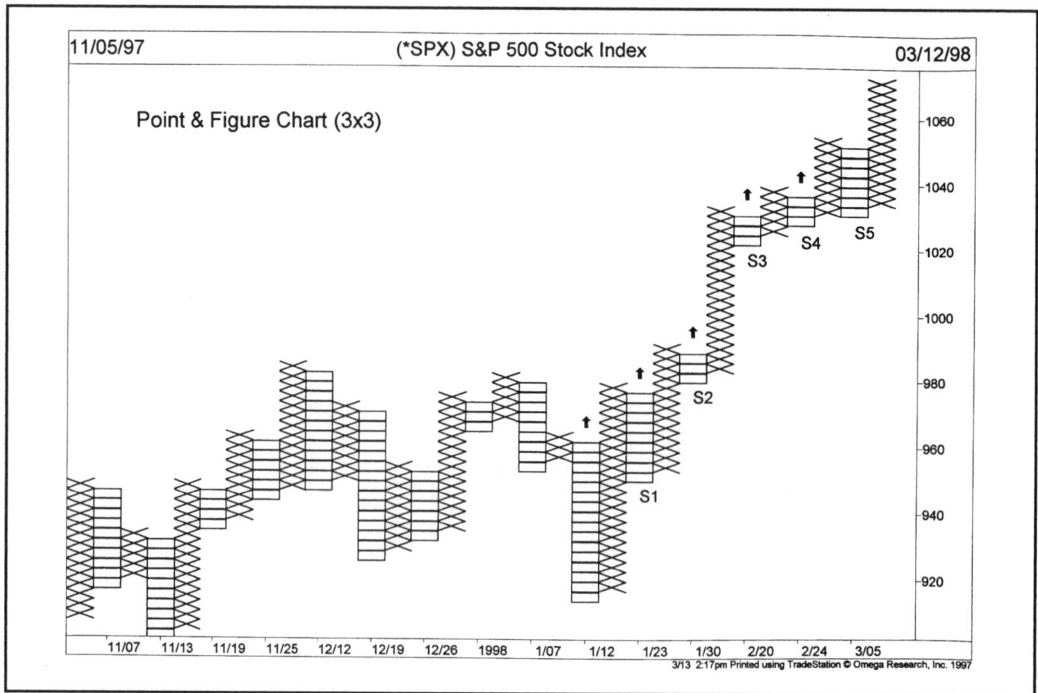

Figure B

1. Figure A is an example of a:
   a. Ten-box reversal.
   b. Five-box reversal.
   c. Three-box reversal.
   d. Triple Top.

2. Figure B is an example of a:
   a. Ten-box reversal.
   b. Five-box reversal.
   c. Three-box reversal.
   d. Profits and profitability chart.

3. Point and figure charts can be made more sensitive by using:
   a. A smaller reversal number.
   b. A larger reversal number.
   c. Time reference points.
   d. The x column.

4. Which is an example of a box size value?

a. 1.00

b. 2.00

c. 5.00

d. All of the above.

5. You see the following on a candlestick chart:

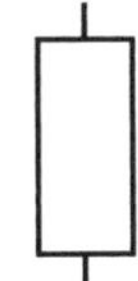

It means:

a. The difference between the close and open prices is small.

b. The close price is lower than the open.

c. The difference between the close and open prices is great.

d. None of the above.

6. The traditional order of reversal criteria is:

a. Three-one-five box reversal.

b. One-two-three box reversal.

c. One-three-five box reversal.

d. Five-three-one box reversal.

7. You look at a chart consisting of the following types of figures:

These are:

a. Long and Short Days.

b. Spinning Tops.

c. Doji candlesticks.

d. reversal patterns.

Refer to the following figure to answer question 8:

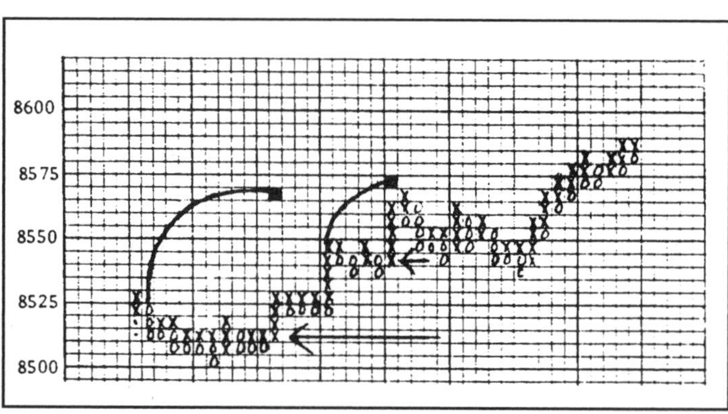

8. This figure depicts:
   a. A one-day cycle.
   b. The problems that congestion areas produce.
   c. Long-term plotting.
   d. How price objectives are determined.

Refer to the following figure to answer question 9:

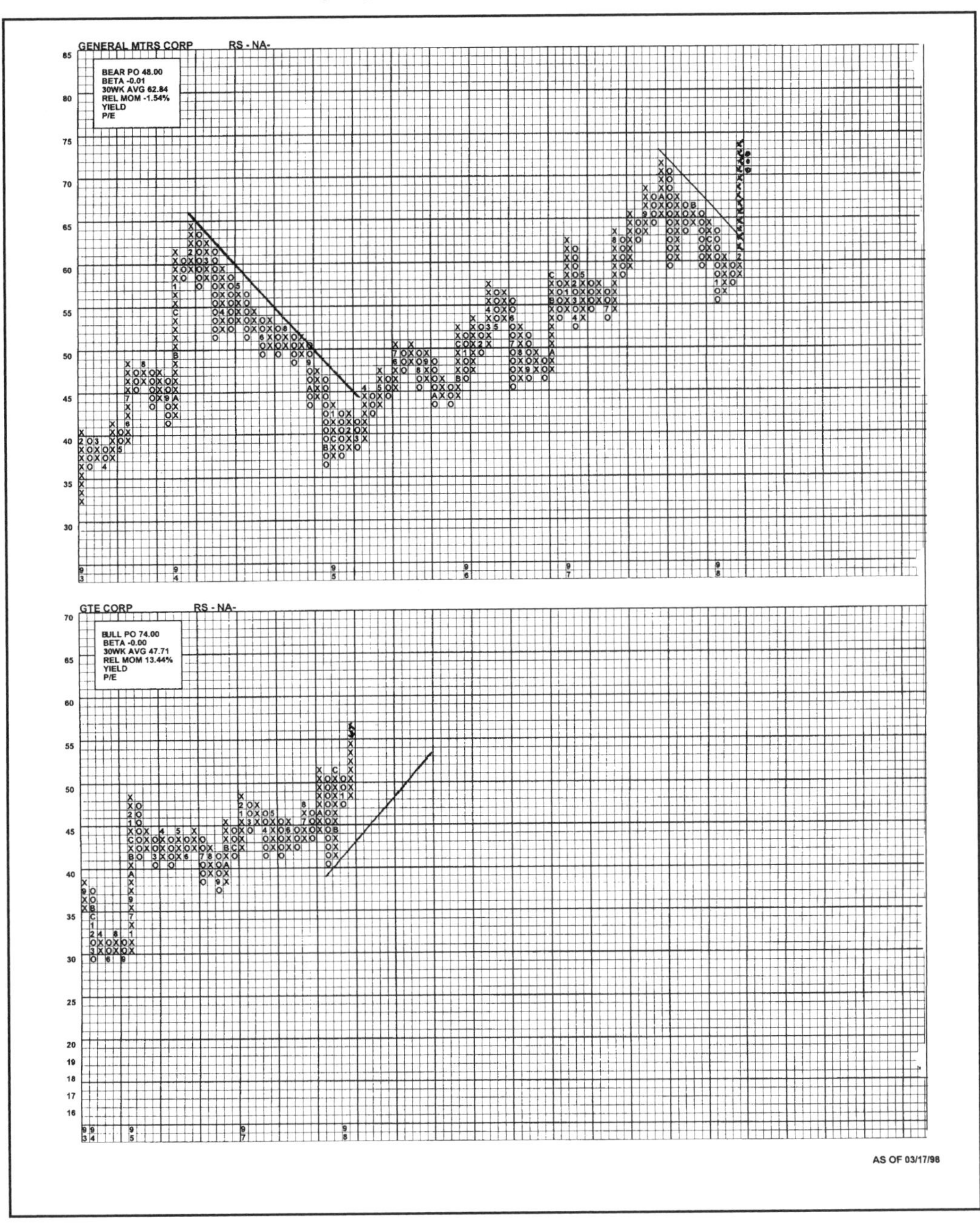

9. The dashed line indicates:
   a. Trendlines always connecting tops and bottoms.
   b. 45-degree trendlines.
   c. A 5-day reversal criterion.
   d. The conventional use of drawing trendlines.

10. When using point and figure charts:
   a. A trendline can be used as a filter.
   b. Short positions are covered on any simple buy signal.
   c. Long positions are liquidated on any simple sell signal.
   d. All of the above.

11. Point and figure charts are ideal in that:
   a. There is only one single box and reversal size.
   b. They have one specific use.
   c. Generalized entry and exit points are sometimes obtainable.
   d. Trading signals are more precise than on bar charts.

Refer to the following figure to answer question 12:

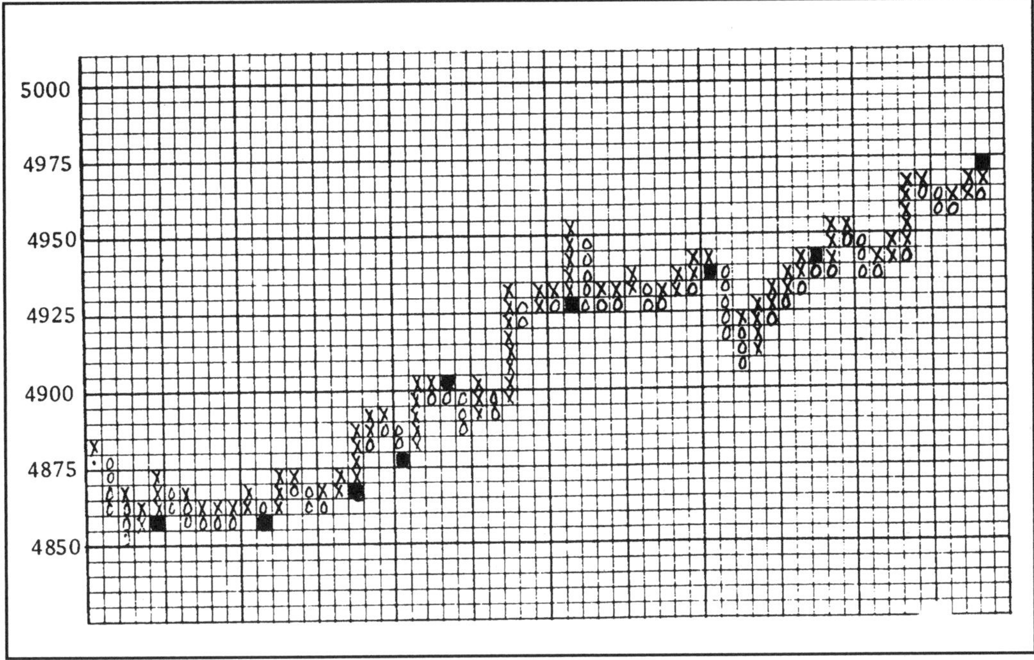

12. In this figure, which statement is most accurate?
    a. The use of X's and O's in the same column never occurs.
    b. This is an example of a three-box reversal.
    c. The blackened boxes are used as reference points.
    d. None of the above.

13. Separating Lines, Upside Tasuki Gap, Three Line Strike, and In Neck all have one thing in common. What is it?
    a. They are bearish reversal patterns.
    b. They are bearish continuation patterns.
    c. They are bullish reversal patterns.
    d. They are bullish continuation patterns.

14. A fulcrum:
    a. Is a congestion area.
    b. Occurs after a significant advance or decline.
    c. Forms an accumulation base or distribution top.
    d. All of the above.

15. The saucer, v extended, delayed ending, and fulcrum all have one thing in common. What is it?
   a. They are continuation patterns.
   b. They are tops.
   c. They are candlestick patterns.
   d. They are bottom reversal patterns.

16. Point and figure charts are designed to measure:
   a. Time and price movement.
   b. Time movement.
   c. Price movement.
   d. Time, price, and breadth movement.

Refer to the following figure to answer question 17:

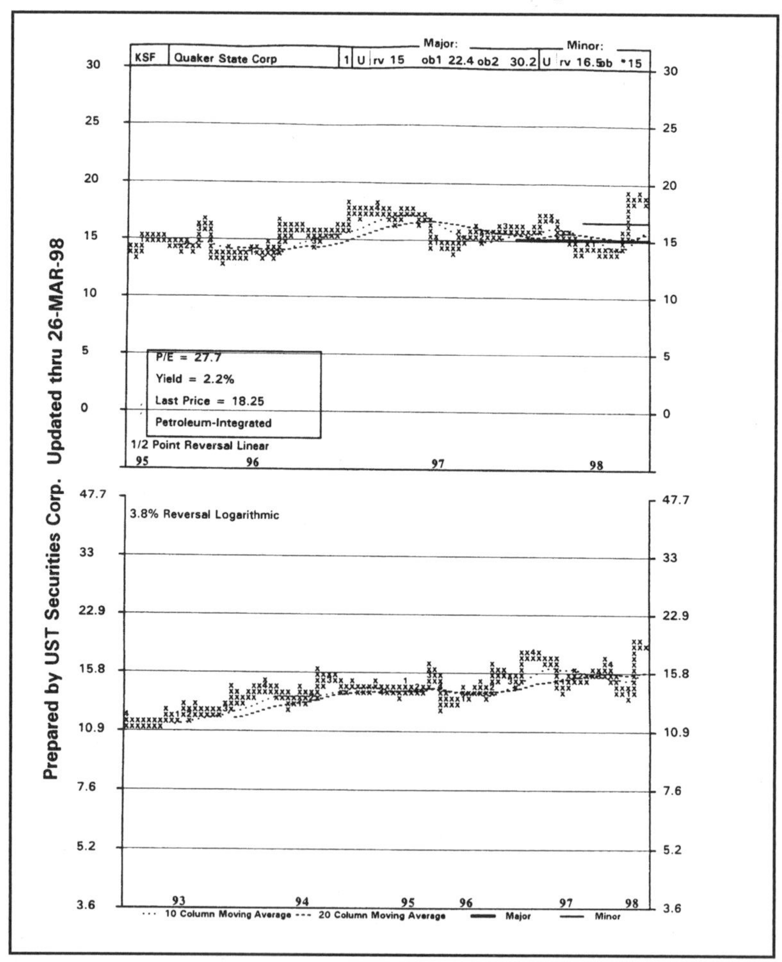

17. The dot and dash lines represent:

a. Volume and open interest.

b. Two moving averages.

c. The difference between open and close prices.

d. None of the above.

ANSWER SHEET

MATCHING QUIZ

A. 20
B. 2
C. 1
D. 15
E. 9
F. 14
G. 18
H. 3
I. 10
J. 11
K. 4
L. 16
M. 21
N. 10
O. 5
P. 12
Q. 7
R. 22
S. 6
T. 25
U. 8
V. 24
W. 23
X. 27
Y. 26

FILL-INS

1. congestion area
2. point and figure chart
3. more
4. Dark Cloud Cover ... Piercing Line
5. shadow ... body
6. white
7. Volume
8. entry ... exit
9. Short
10. pole
11. support ... resistance
12. intraday point and figure chart
13. Doji candlesticks

MULTIPLE CHOICE

1. **c** This is an example of a three-box reversal. There is no indication of a triple top formation. See Figure 11.3, page 269.
2. **c** This is an example of a three-box reversal employing the point and figure method of charting. See Figure 11.4, page 269.
3. **a** Sensitivity occurs by smaller reversal numbers. Reference points are selected by the user. They are not part of determining price movements in point and figure charts. The x column is used for plotting purposes. See page 270.
4. **d** All of the listed values can be used to determine box sizes. The larger the box value, the less sensitive the chart. See page 270.
5. **c** A short body indicates a small difference. A dark body means the close was lower than the open. See page 300.
6. **c** Traditionally, the order used is to begin with the one-box reversal chart and then move to the three- and five-box reversal. See page 273.
7. **c** Options a and b relate to body/shadow candlestick formations. See page 300–301.
8. **d** This figure demonstrates how price objectives are determined. The analyst counts the number of columns across the horizontal congestion area in order to determine price objectives. See Figure 11.6, page 275.

9. **b** The dashed lines in this figure depict 45-degree trendlines. They are used only on the three-box reversal charts. This is not a 5-day reversal chart. The 45-degree line is not a conventional way to draw trendlines. Because of the severe condensation on these charts, it's impractical to connect tops and bottoms. See Figure 11.11, page 284.
10. **d** Trendlines are used as filters on point and figure charts. Choices b and c are true—short positions are covered on a simple buy signal. See page 282-286.
11. **d** Because of their design, point and figure charts are much more precise than bar charts in terms of trading signals. Box and reversal sizes can and do vary. There are many different ways these charts are used for entry and exit points. Entry and exit points are also specific on these charts. See page 266-270.
12. **c** This figure is a one-box reversal chart which allows x's and o's to occupy the same column. The blackened boxes identify the end of each day's trading. See page 272.
13. **d** See "Candle Patterns" on page 309.
14. **d** The term "fulcrum" (or "congestion area") includes in its definition all of the listed choices. This is a fairly common occurrence in point and figure charting. See page 275.
15. **d** See Figure 11.7, page 276.
16. **c** Point and figure charts are meant to record pure price movement and not time. In fact, these charts ignore time. See page 266.
17. **b** While moving averages are used more often on bar charts, they can be applied to point and figure charts. See Figure 11.21 on page 294, 295.

Final Assessment

The purpose of this assessment is to evaluate your grasp of the basic concepts and techniques of technical analysis. The questions are designed to take you a step further than the lesson questions, by requiring you to apply your knowledge to actual charts. The assessment itself should be part of the learning experience.

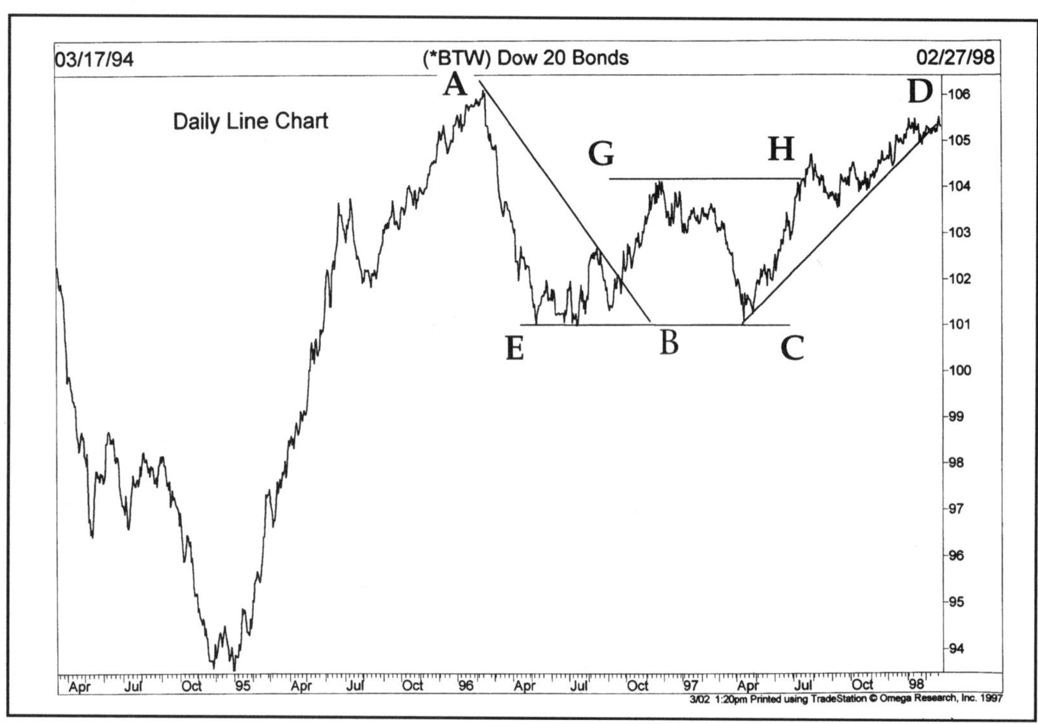

Questions 1–5 refer to FIGURE 1:

1. A resistance line would run between points _________ and _________.

2. The up trendline would be drawn between points _________ and _________.

3. The down trendline would be drawn between points _________ and _________.

4. A support line would run between points _________ and _________.

5. The breakout is taking place at point _____.

Questions 6–10 refer to FIGURE 2:

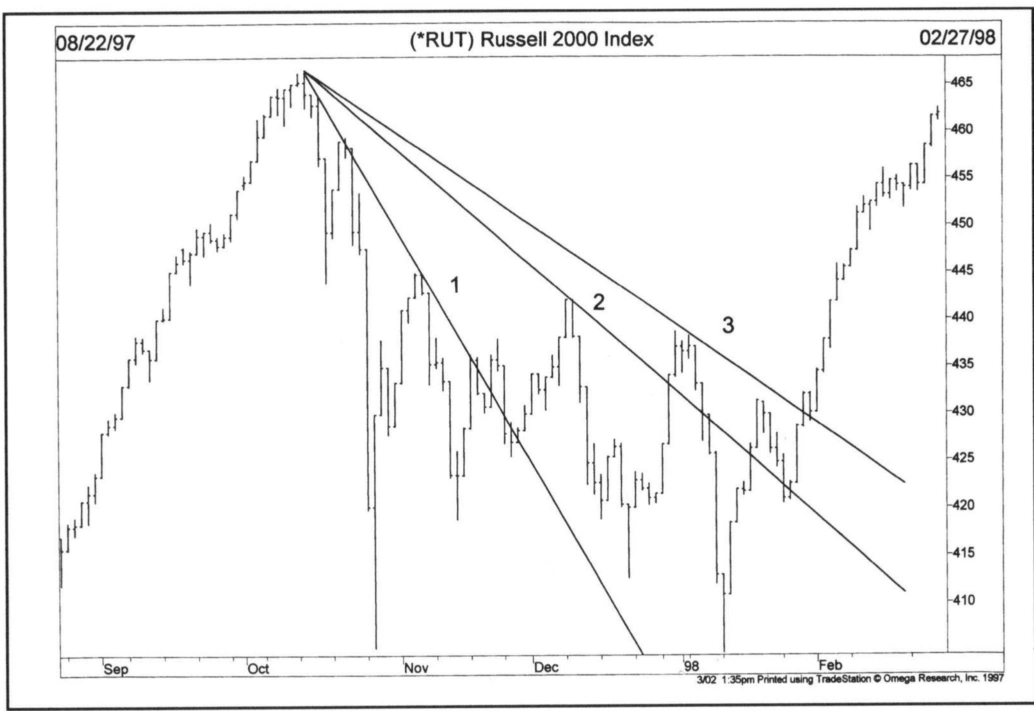

6. This is a bar/line/point and figure/candlestick chart.
7. The three divergent trendlines are _________ _________.
8. A reversal and a buy signal occur when prices move upward through which line? _________
9. Each line can be described as a support/resistance line.
10. Once broken, each line can become a support/resistance line.

Questions 11–15 refer to FIGURE 3:

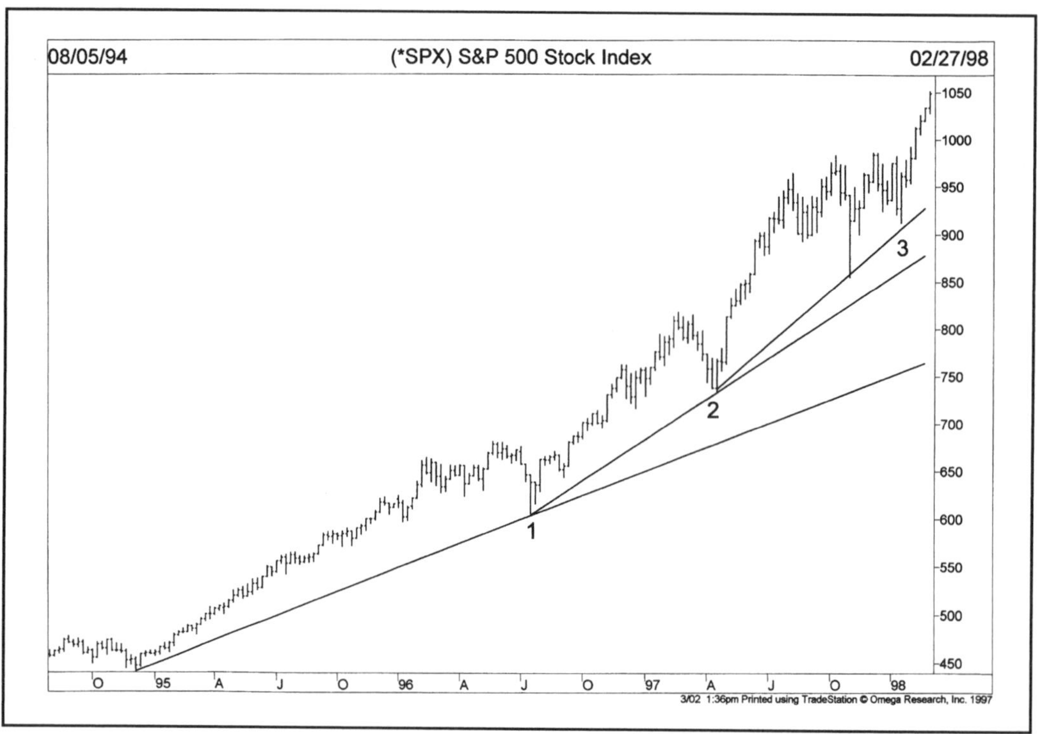

11. The chart is a daily/weekly bar chart.

12. The major, or primary, trendline is number _________.

13. The short-term advance is shown by trendline number _________.

14. The intermediate trendline is number _________.

15. If any of the trendlines were to exceed 45 degrees, it may be unsustainable/irreversible.

Questions 16–20 refer to FIGURE 4:

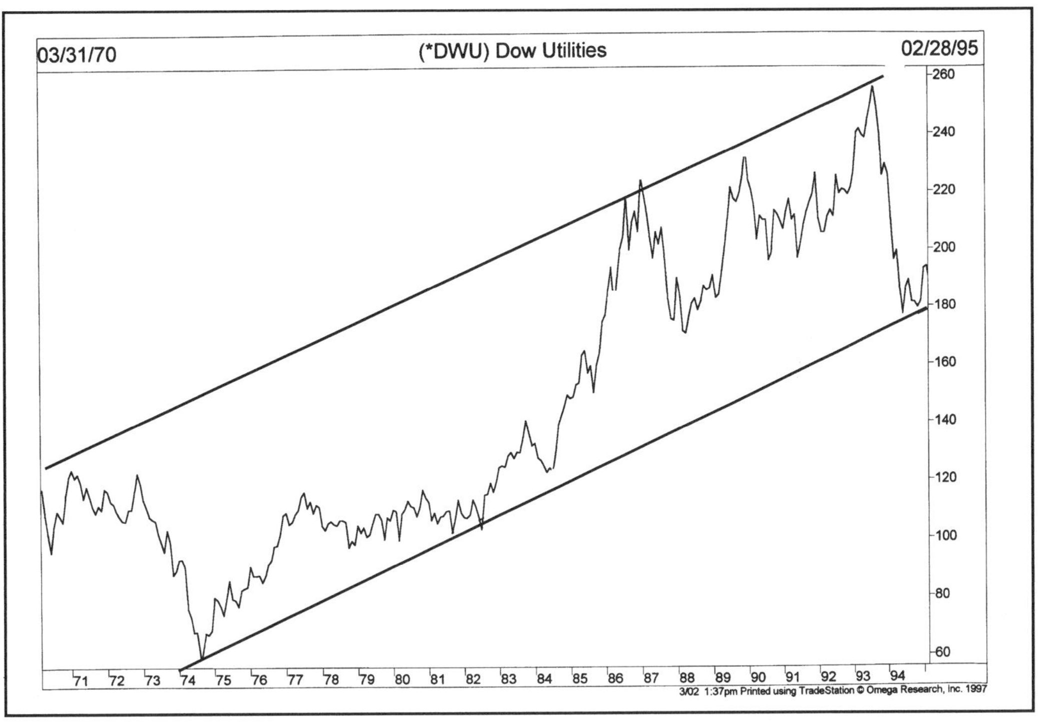

16. The chart is a weekly/monthly line/bar point and figure chart.

17. The two parallel lines are ____________________ __________.

18. If prices fail to reach the upper line, you would expect the trend to weaken/strengthen.

19. If prices were to break through the upper line, you would expect a(n) change/acceleration in the uptrend.

20. Given a breakout, prices usually travel a distance equal to the width/one-half the width/one-third the width of the channel.

Questions 21–24 refer to FIGURE 5:

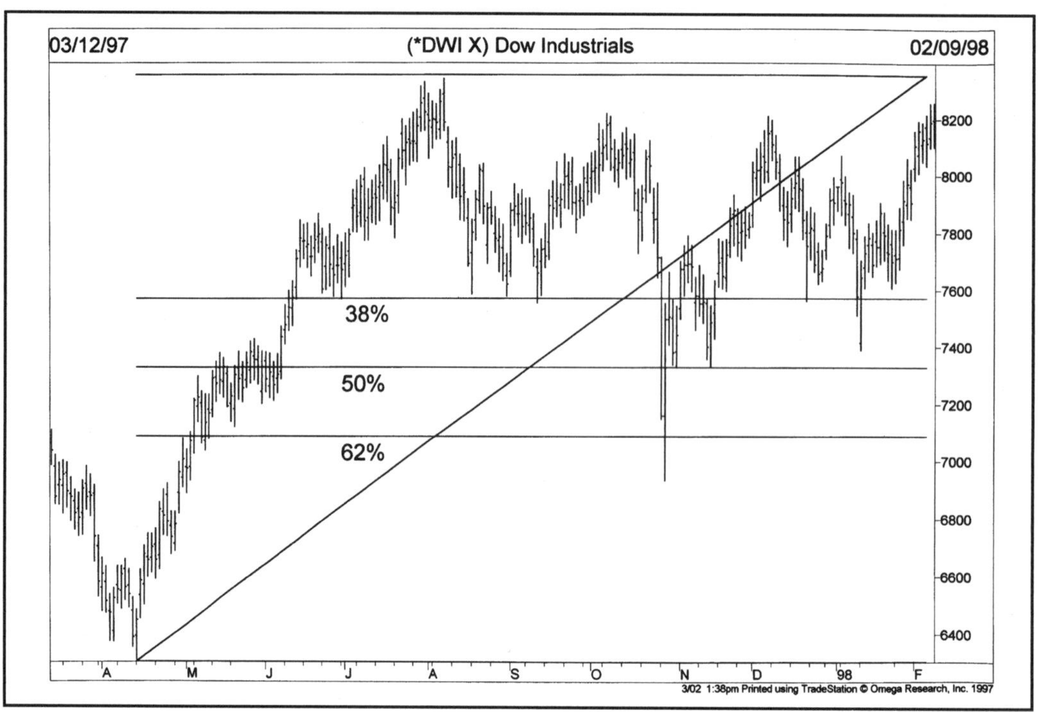

21. The chart is a daily/weekly bar chart.

22. The horizontal lines represent percentages of ________________.

23. Each line represents a ________________ equal to a percentage of the distance from the low in April to the high in August.

24. The three lines reflect recognition of the fact that a price trend can be broken down into quarters/thirds/halves.

Questions 25–28 refer to Figure 6:

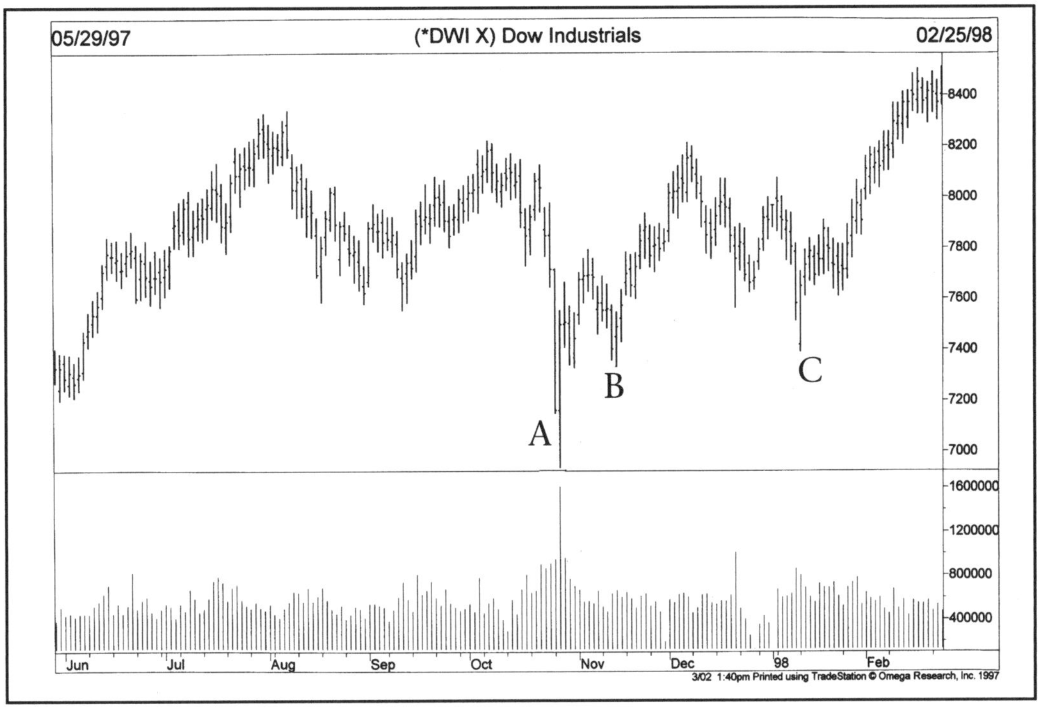

25. The chart is a daily/weekly bar chart.

26. The vertical lines at the bottom of the chart represent ______________.

27. A dramatic selling climax occurs at point _________.

28. That selling climax differs from the other two points because it is accompanied by heavy __________________.

Questions 29–34 refer to FIGURES 7a and b:

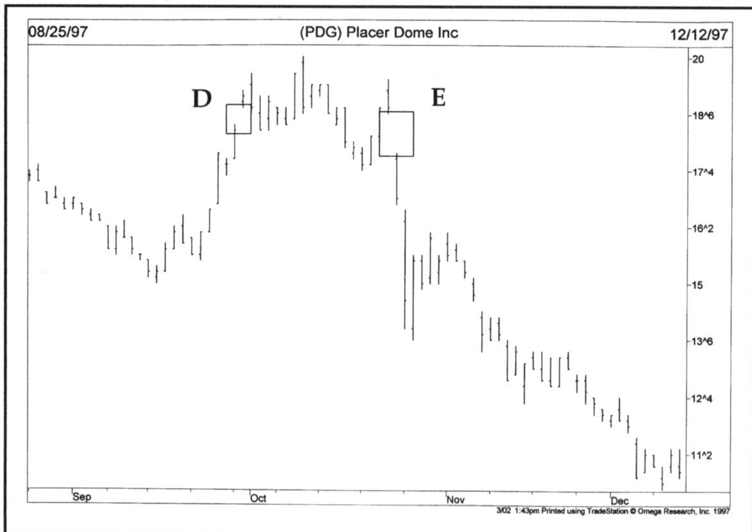

29. Point A is what kind of gap? ____________________

30. Point B is what kind of gap? ____________________

31. Point C is what kind of gap? ____________________

32. Point D is what kind of gap? ____________________ ______

33. Point E is what kind of gap? ____________________ ______

34. Points D and E, in combination, signal a(n) ______________ ______________ _________.

Questions 35–39 refer to FIGURE 8:

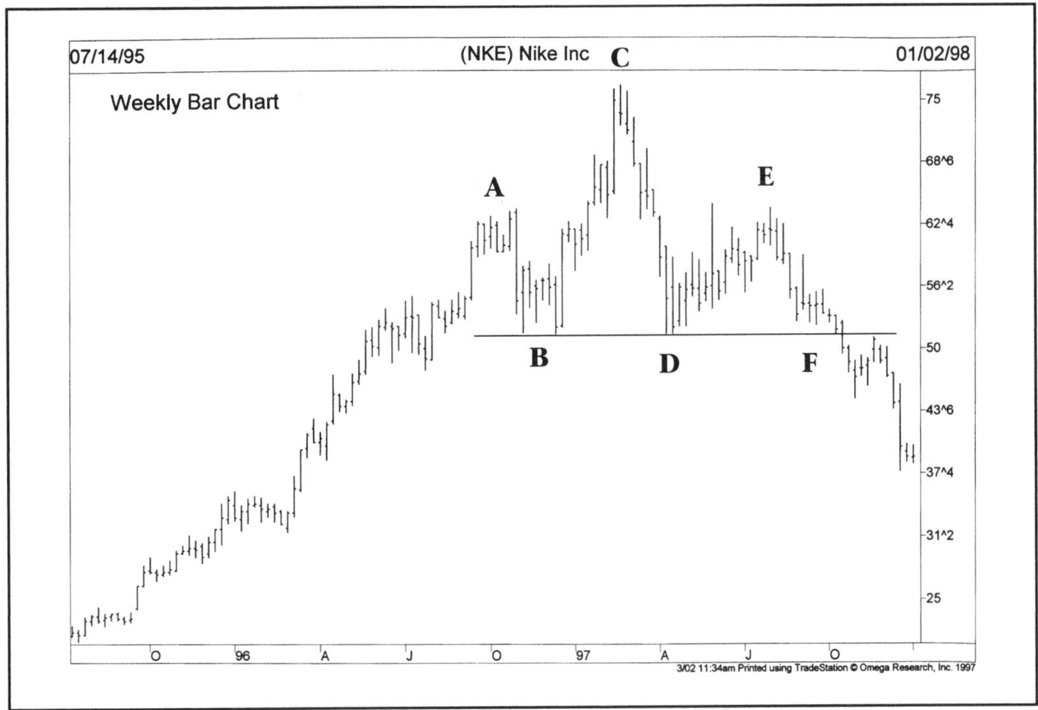

35. The pattern in the figure is a __________ __________ __________.

36. The horizontal line is called the ________________.

37. This is a continuation/reversal pattern.

38. The pattern is considered decisive at point ________.

39. Volume is probably going to be greatest at point ________.

Questions 40–43 refer to FIGURE 9:

40. The pattern between points A and B is a ____________________ ____________________.

41. The pattern may be considered bullish/bearish.

42. The breakout (at point B), about two-thirds of the way through the pattern, is common/atypical.

43. This is a reversal/continuation pattern.

Questions 44–55 refer to FIGURE 10:

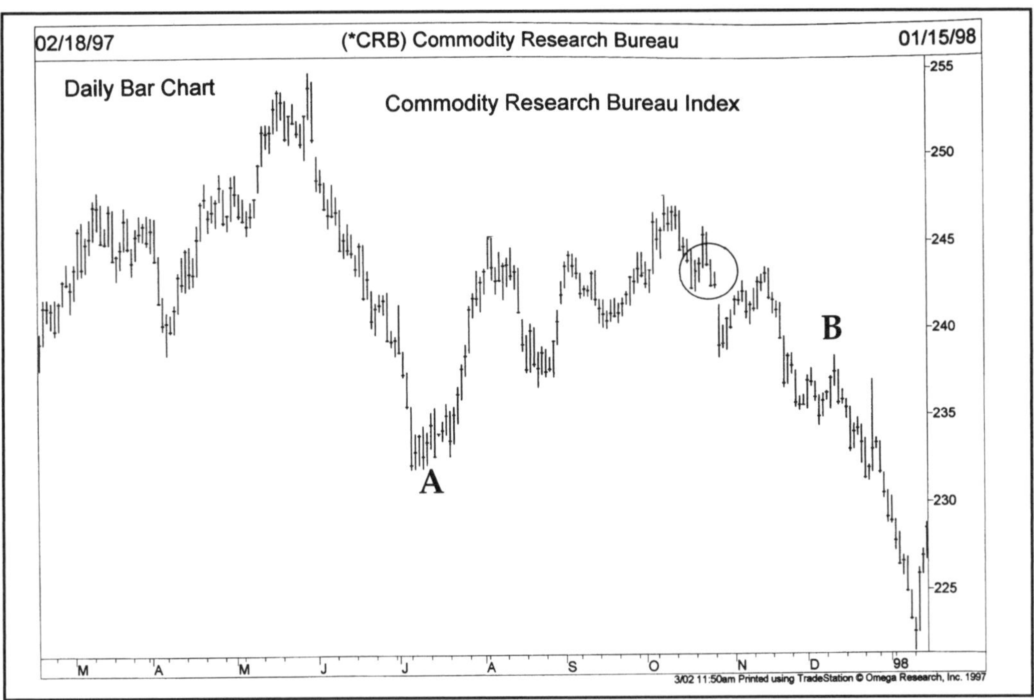

44. The pattern between points A and B is a ______________ ______________.

45. It is usually a bullish/bearish pattern.

Questions 46–50 refer to FIGURE 11:

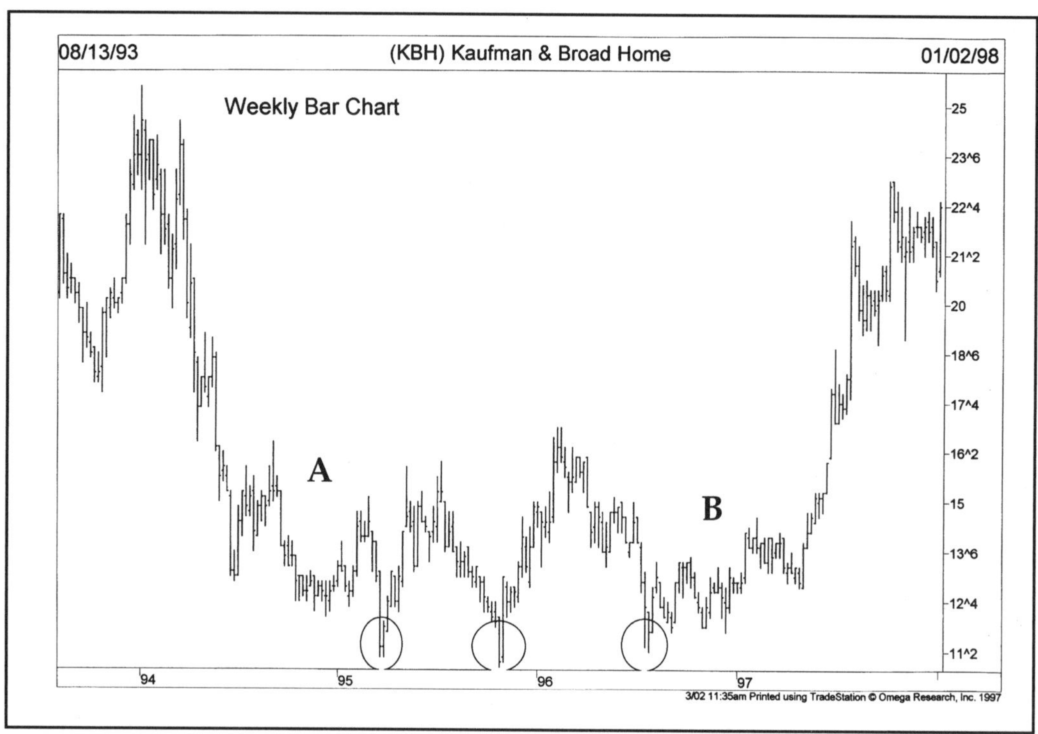

46. The pattern between points A and B is a ______________ ______________.

47. It is a reversal/continuation pattern.

48. This pattern is bullish/bearish.

49. Prices may move as much as the full height/one-half/one-third of the pattern.

50. A return move to the breakout point is likely/not possible.

Questions 51–53 refer to FIGURE 12:

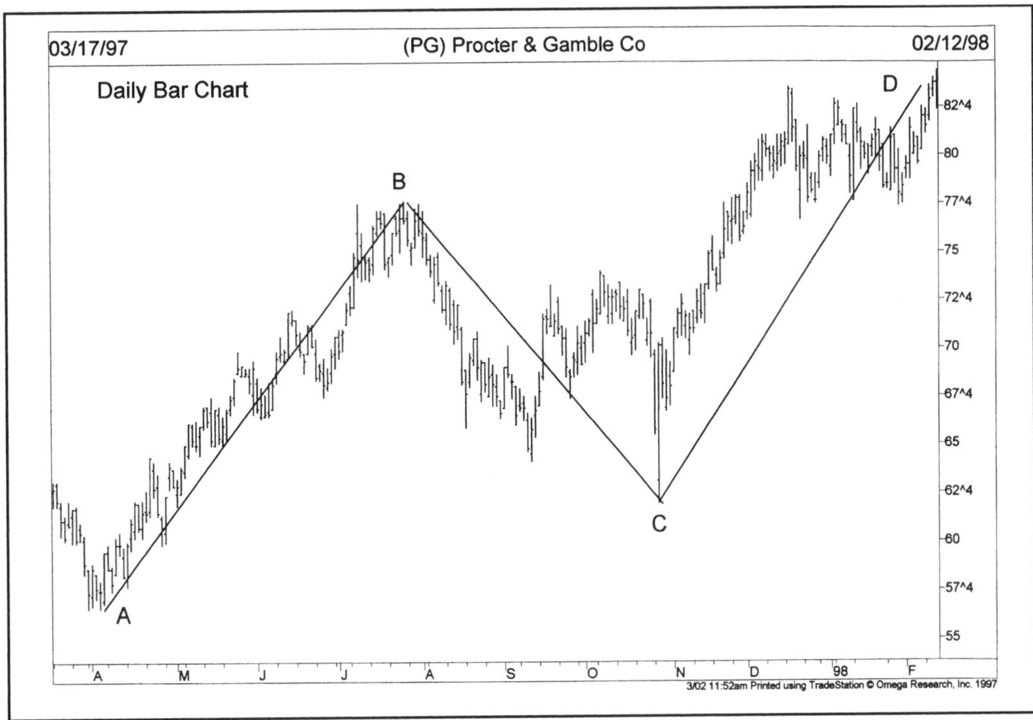

51. The pattern drawn by the four lines is a ________________ ________________.

52. The line BC may retrace up to how much of line AB? ________________

53. The line CD may be expected to be as long as/longer than line AB.

Questions 54–57 refer to FIGURE 13:

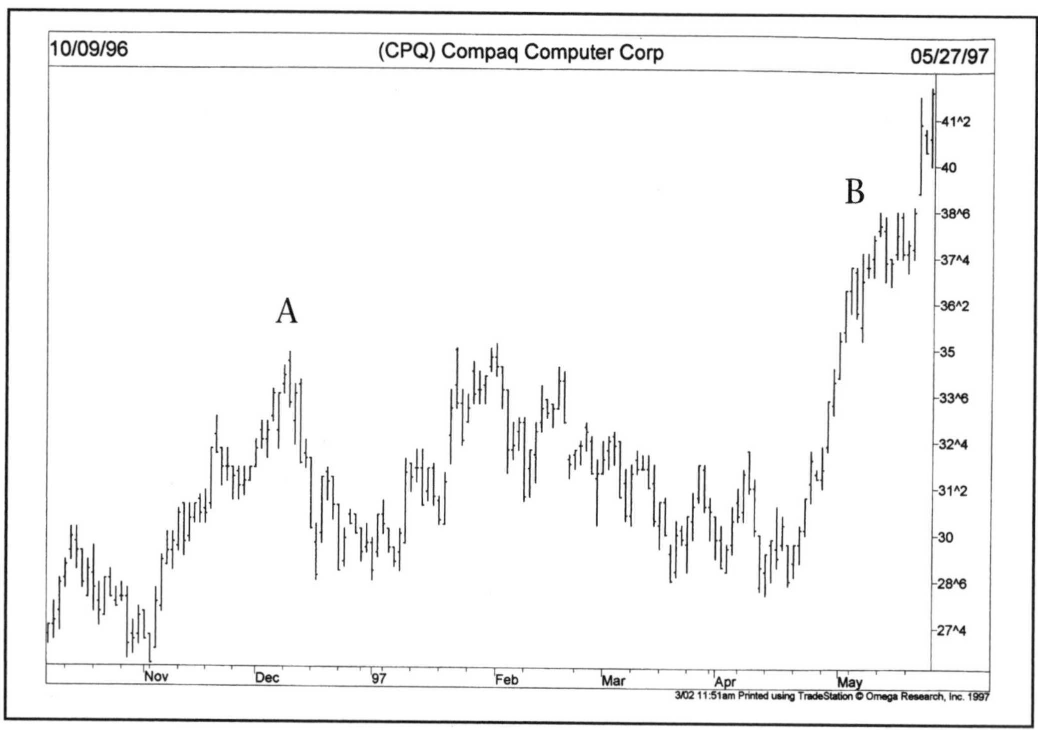

54. The pattern between points A and B is a ________________.

55. It is bullish/bearish.

56. Another name for this pattern is

______________________________.

57. Once prices breakout, they may be expected to move how far?

____

Questions 58–60 refer to FIGURE 14:

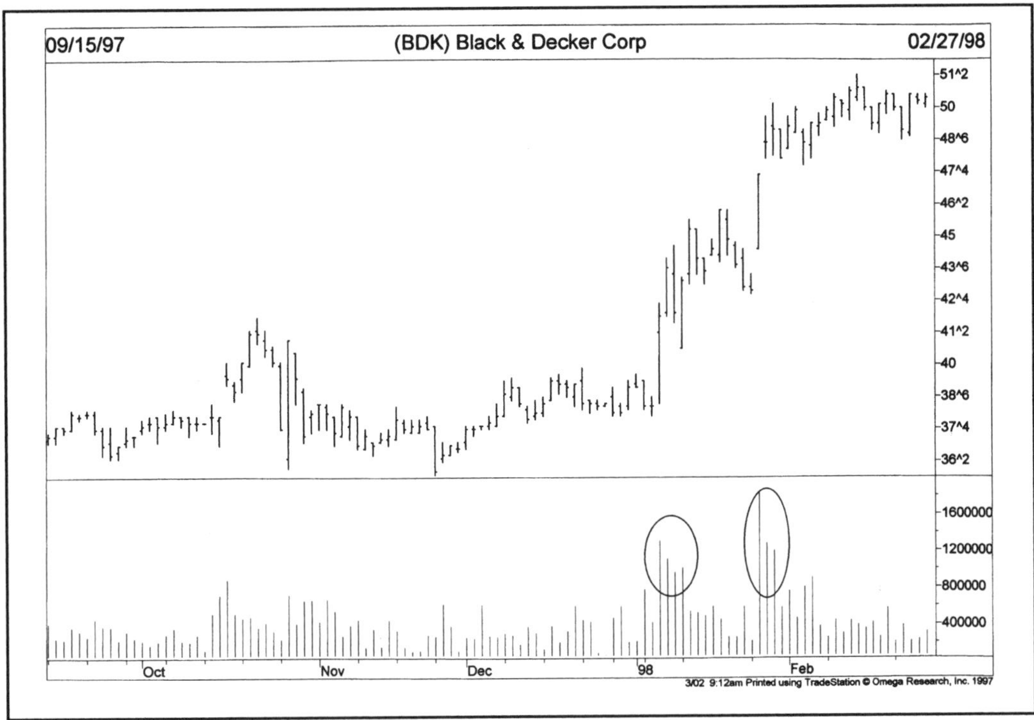

58. The vertical lines at the bottom of the chart represent ____________________.

59. The vertical lines in the circles, in relation to the price movements alone, are said to be confirming/divergent.

60. This is a short-/medium-/long-term chart.

Questions 61–63 refer to FIGURE 15:

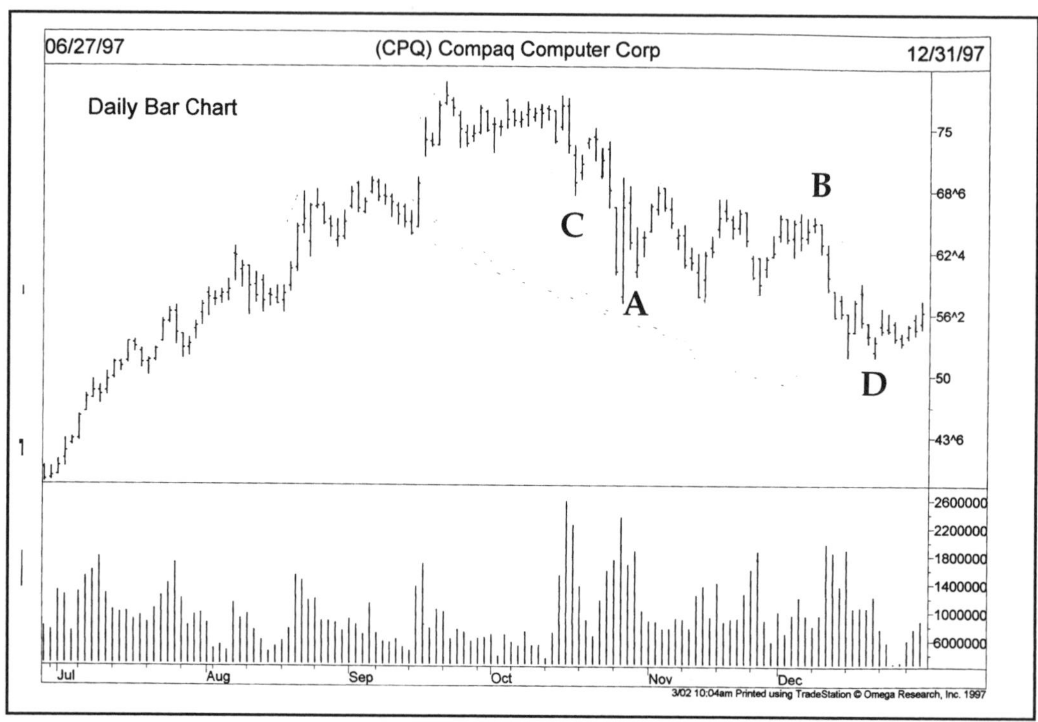

61. The pattern between points A and B is a ____________________.

62. It is a reversal/continuation pattern.

63. The downturns at points C and D are both accompanied by ______________ ______________.

Question 64 refers to FIGURE 16:

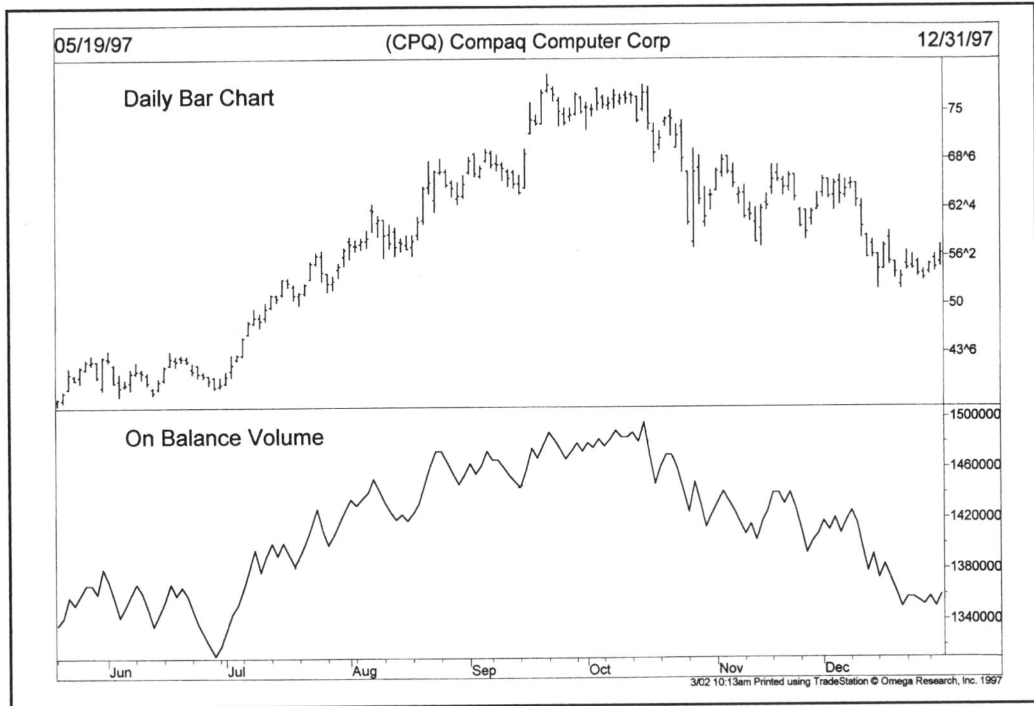

64. If the line at the bottom of the chart follows prices, it is said to confirm/diverge from the price movements.

Questions 65–67 refer to FIGURE 17:

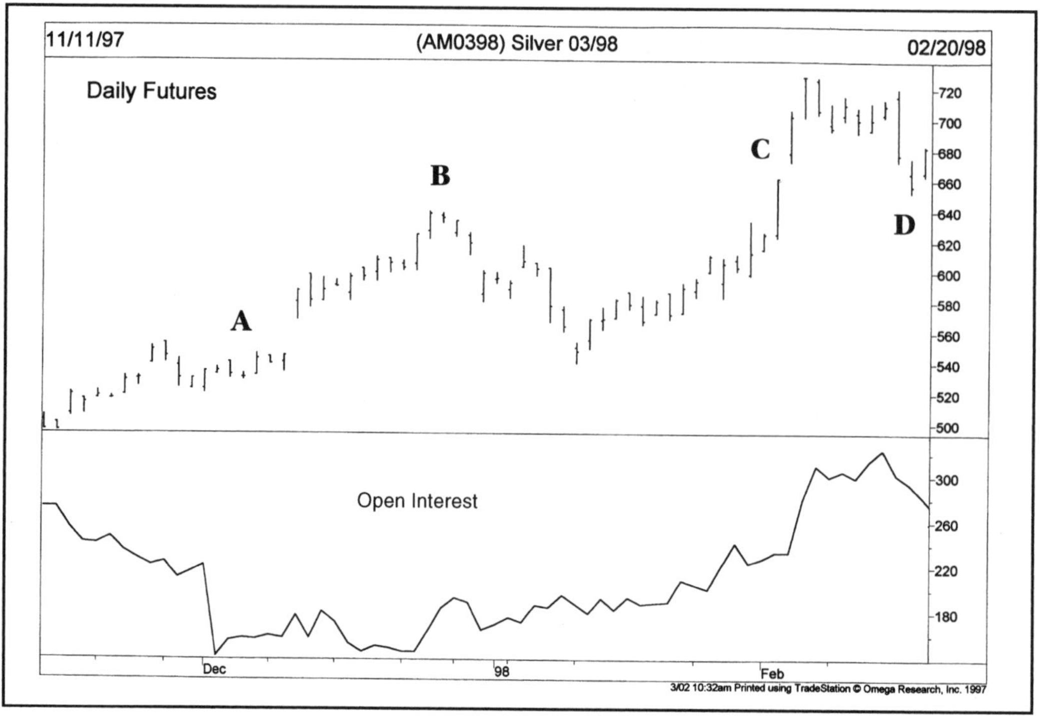

65. The line at the bottom of the chart represents the total number of ______________ ______________ or ______________.

66. At which point is new money—new buyers—coming into the market? ________

67. At which point are contracts being liquidated as prices start to correct downward? ________

Questions 68–71 refer to FIGURE 18:

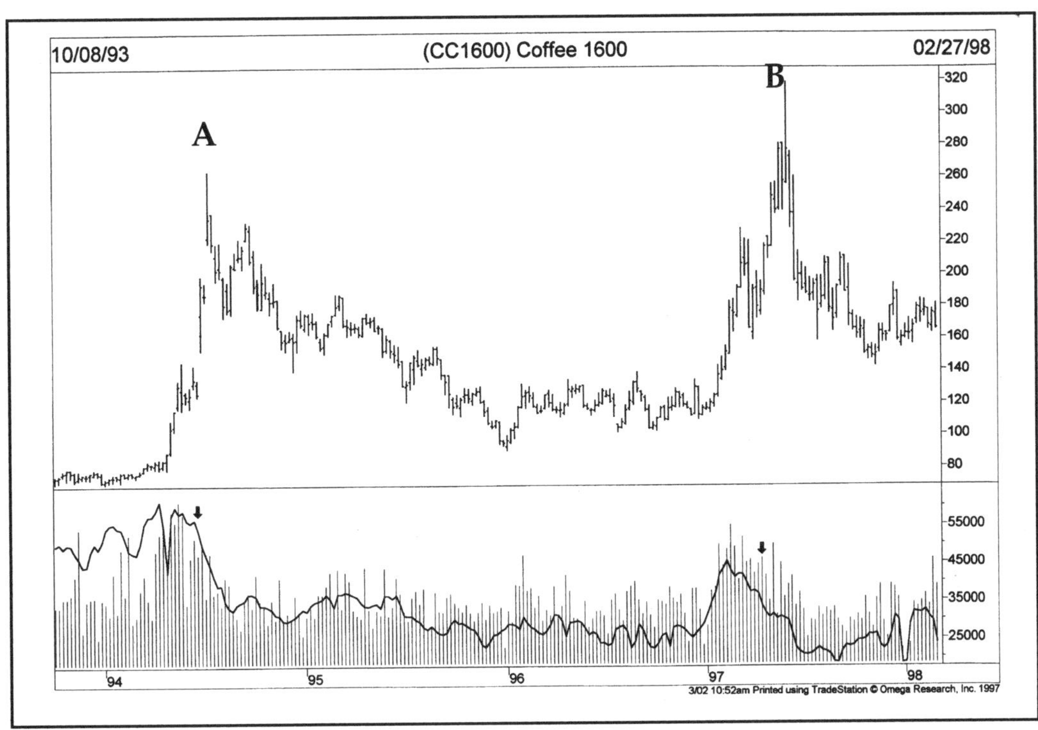

68. Points A and B are called ____________________.

69. If these patterns were to occur at market bottoms, they would be called ____________________ ____________________.

70. During both patterns, volume was light/heavy.

71. During both patterns, open interest declined/increased.

Questions 72–75 refer to FIGURE 19:

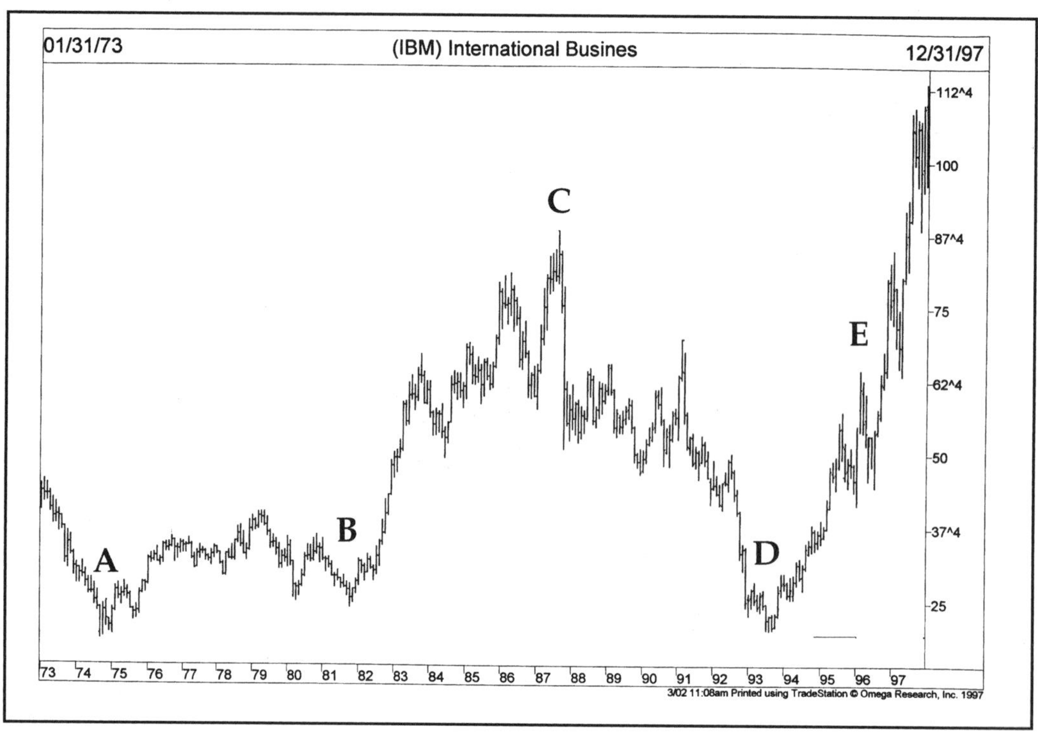

72. The chart is a weekly/monthly bar chart.

73. Long-term support can be found at roughly what level? __________

74. Which point(s) demonstrate the support level? __________

75. Which point indicates the start of a major new trend? __________

Questions 76–79 refer to FIGURE 20:

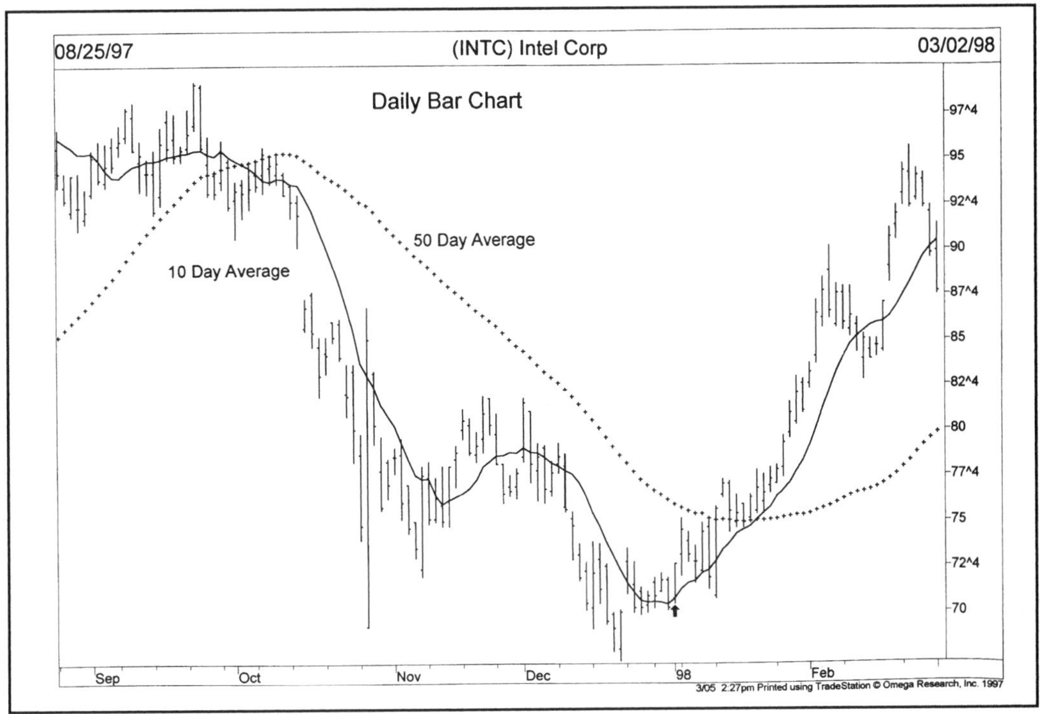

76. The two moving average lines represent an averaging of price/volume data.

77. The 10 Day Average is said to be shorter/longer than the 50 Day Average.

78. The 10 Day Average/50 Day Average signaled the market upturn first.

79. The 10 Day Average/50 Day Average gave a premature buy signal before the upturn.

Questions 80–82 refer to FIGURE 21:

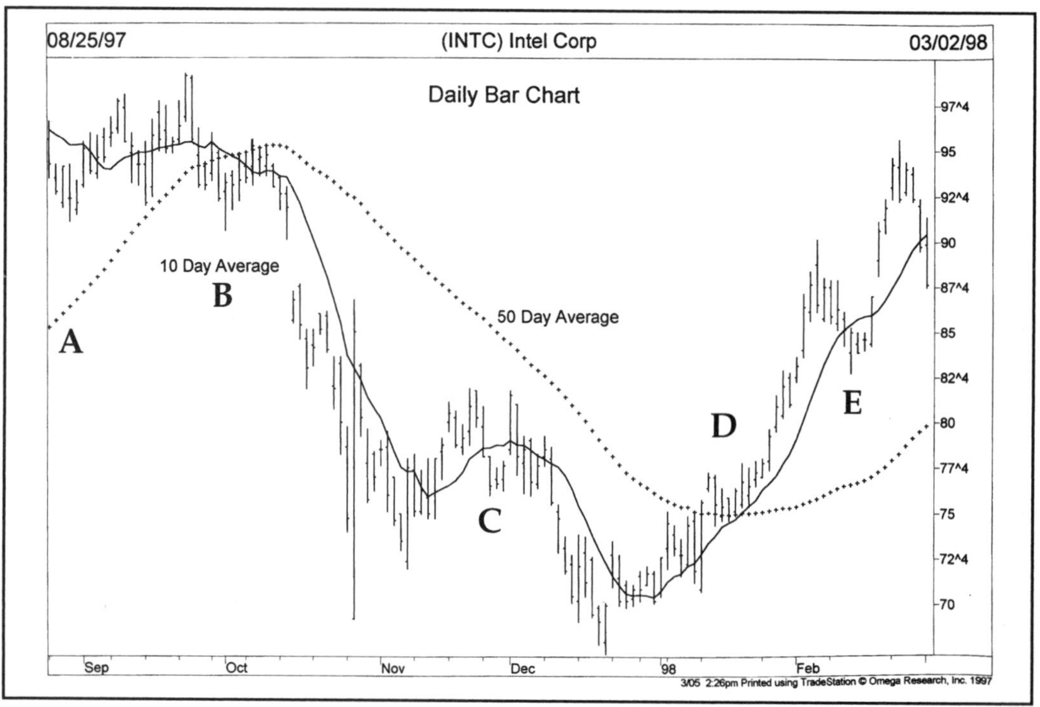

80. Point(s) ________ demonstrate(s) the double crossover method.

81. Point ________ is a sell signal.

82. Point ________ is a buy signal.

Questions 83–85 refer to FIGURE 22:

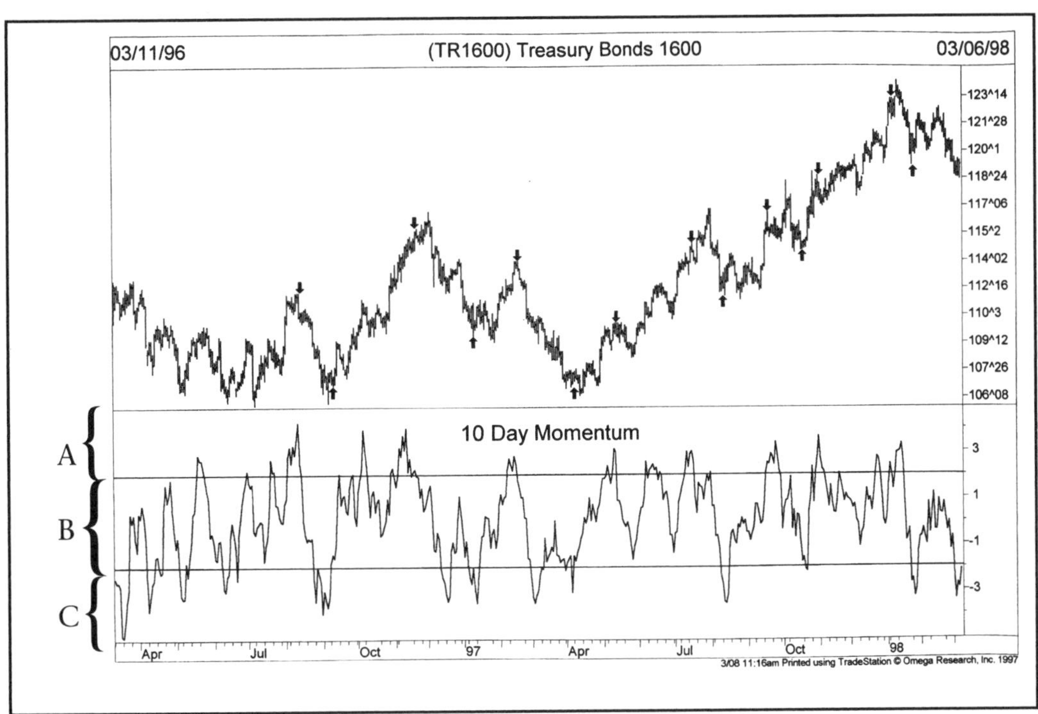

83. The curve at the bottom of the chart is a(n) ____________________.

84. In range __________, this market is said to be overbought.

85. In range __________, this market is said to be oversold.

Questions 86–88 refer to FIGURE 23:

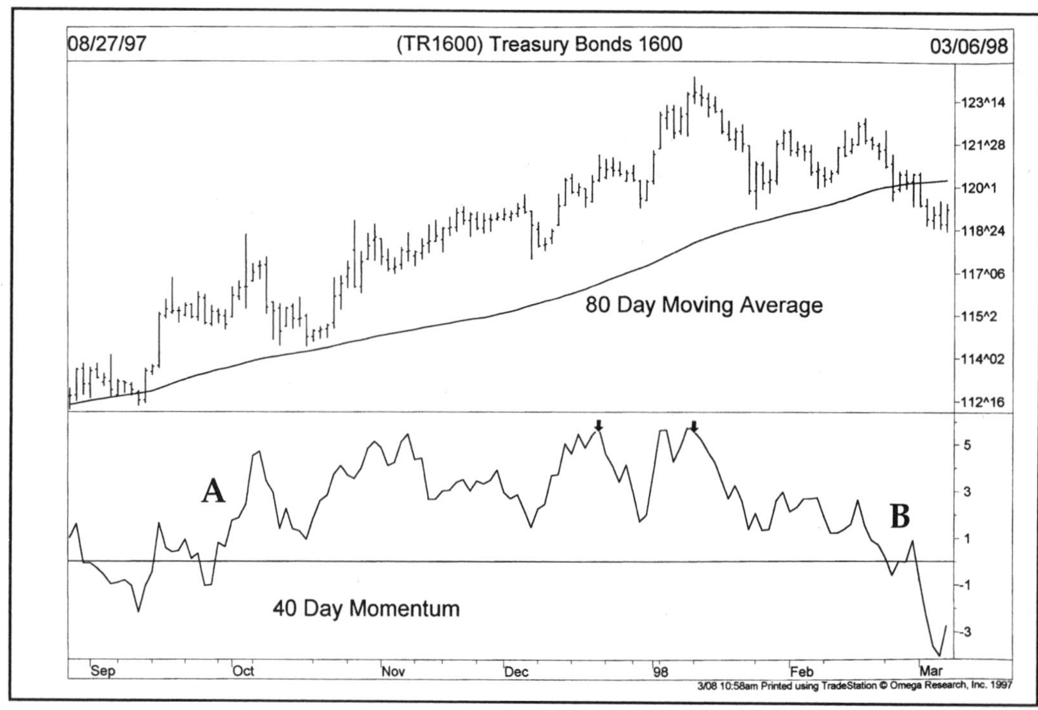

86. The horizontal line running through the oscillator at the bottom of the chart is called the __________ __________.

87. Point A, a crossing above the line, is a buy/sell signal.

88. Point B, a crossing below the line, is a buy/sell signal.

Questions 89–91 refer to FIGURE 24:

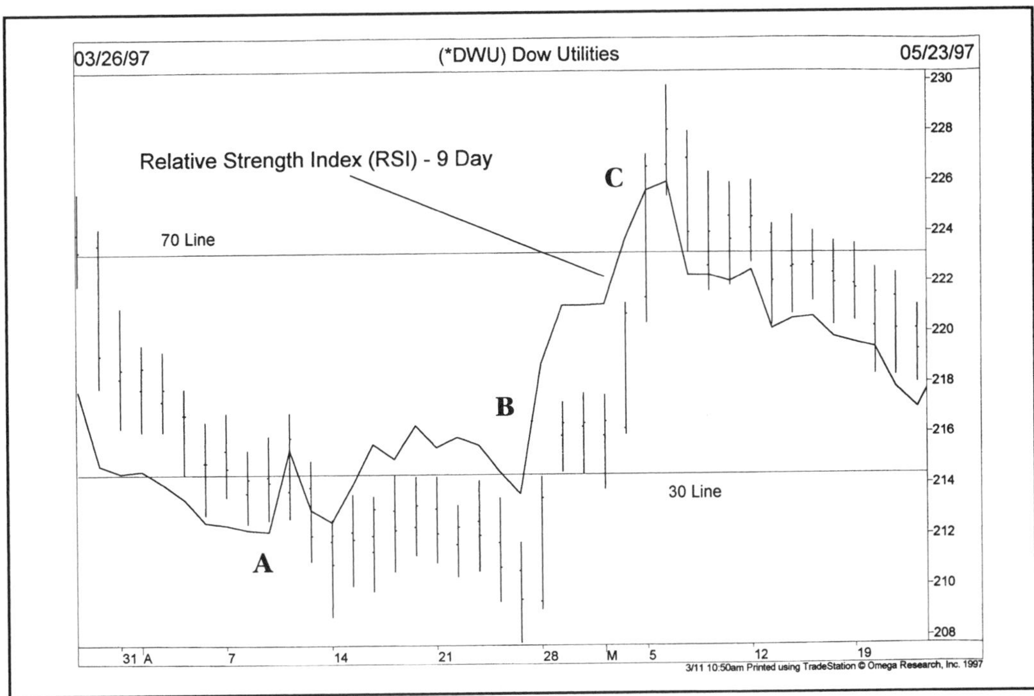

89. The RSI line represents a ratio determined by dividing the ____________________ by the ____________________ of price moves.

90. The chart demonstrates a bottom/top failure swing.

91. Point __________ signals a bottom.

Questions 92–96 refer to FIGURE 25:

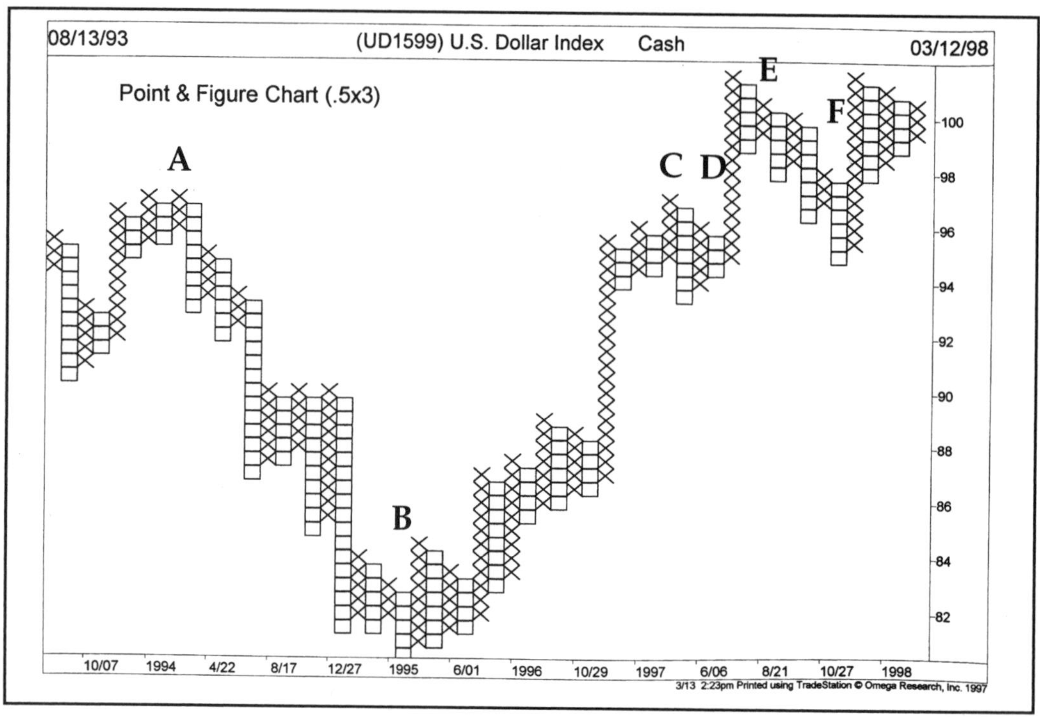

92. In this chart, each box is equal to .5/.3.

93. The reversal criterion is 5/3.

94. Buy signals occur at point(s) ______________.

95. Sell signals occur at point(s) ______________.

96. If the reversal criterion were increased, the chart would be more/less sensitive to price movements.

Questions 97–101 refer to FIGURE 26:

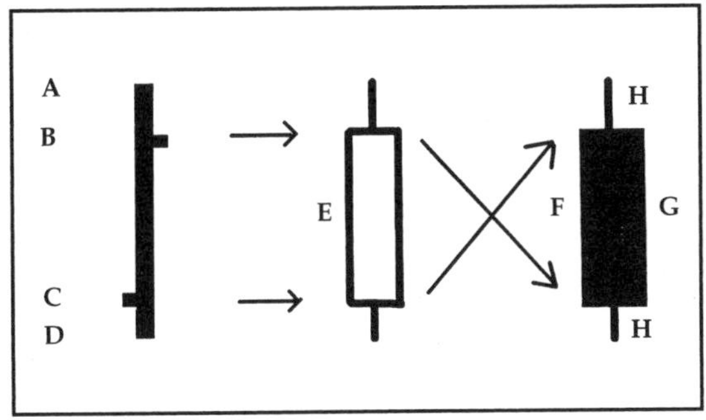

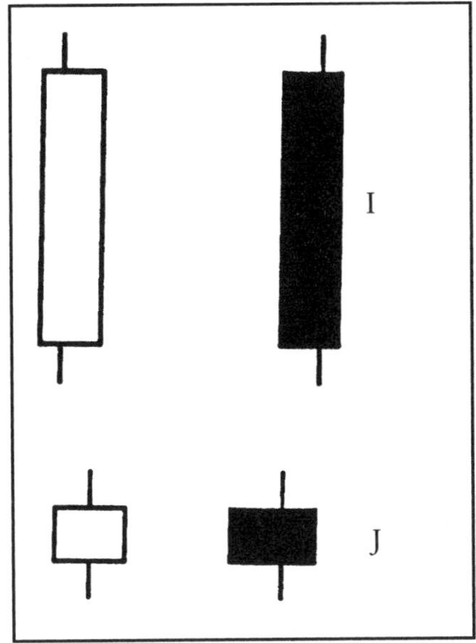

97. The close price is found at point __________.

98. When the close price is lower than the open price, the candlestick used would look like __________.

99. The body is represented by __________.

100. The shadow (wick or hair) is shown by __________.

101. Long Days are reflected by __________.

Final Assessment Answer Sheet

FIGURE 1

1. A resistance line would run between points *G* and *H*.
2. The up trendline would be drawn between points *C* and *D*.
3. The down trendline would be drawn between points *A* and *B*.
4. A support line would run between points *E* and *C*.
5. The breakout is taking place at point *H*.

FIGURE 2

6. This is a *bar* chart.
7. The three divergent trendlines are *fan lines*.

8. A reversal and a buy signal occur when prices move upward through which line? *3*

9. Each line can be described as a *resistance* line.

10. Once broken, each line can become a *support* line.

FIGURE 3

11. The chart is a *weekly* bar chart.

12. The major, or primary trendline is number *1.*

13. The short-term advance is shown by trendline number *3.*

14. The intermediate trendline is number *2.*

15. If the angle of any of the trendlines were to exceed 45 degrees, it may be *unsustainable.*

FIGURE 4

16. The chart is a *monthly line* chart.

17. The two parallel lines are *channel (return) lines.*

18. If prices fail to reach the upper line, you would expect the trend to *weaken.*

19. If prices were to break through the upper line, you would expect a(n) *acceleration* in the uptrend.

20. Given a breakout, prices usually travel a distance equal to the *width* of the channel.

FIGURE 5

21. The chart is a *daily* bar chart.

22. The horizontal lines represent percentages of *retracement.*

23. Each line represents a *correction* equal to a percentage of the distance from the low in April to the high in August.

24. The three lines reflect recognition of the fact that a price trend can be broken down into *thirds.*

FIGURE 6

25. The chart is a *daily* bar chart.

26. The vertical lines at the bottom of the chart represent *volume.*

27. A dramatic selling climax occurs at point *A.*

28. That selling climax differs from the other two points because it is accompanied by heavy *volume.*

FIGURE 7

29. Point A is what kind of gap? *exhaustion*

30. Point B is what kind of gap? *measurement*

31. Point C is what kind of gap? *exhaustion*

32. Point D is what kind of gap? *exhaustion*

33. Point E is what kind of gap? *downside breakaway*

34. Points D and E, in combination, signal a(n) *island reversal top.*

FIGURE 8

35. The pattern in the figure is a *head and shoulders.*
36. The horizontal line is called the *neckline.*
37. This is a *reversal* pattern.
38. The pattern is considered decisive at point *F.*
39. Volume is probably going to be greatest at point *F.*

FIGURE 9

40. The pattern between points A and B is a *symmetrical triangle.*
41. The pattern may be considered *bullish.*
42. The breakout (in the circle), about two-thirds of the way through the pattern, is *common.*
43. This is a *continuation* pattern.

FIGURE 10

44. The pattern between points A and B is a *rising wedge.*
45. It is usually a *bearish* pattern.

FIGURE 11

46. The pattern between point A and B is a *triple bottom.*
47. It is a *reversal* pattern.
48. This pattern is *bullish.*
49. Prices may move as much as the *full height* of the pattern.
50. A return move to the breakout point is *likely.*

FIGURE 12

51. The pattern drawn by the four lines is a *measured move.*
52. The line BC may retrace up to how much of line AB? $\frac{1}{2}$ *to* $\frac{2}{3}$
53. The line CD may be expected to be *as long as* line AB.

FIGURE 13

54. The pattern between points A and B is a *rectangle.*
55. It is *bullish.*
56. Another name for this pattern is *trading range/congestion area.*
57. Once prices breakout, they may be expected to move how far? *The height of the pattern*

FIGURE 14

58. The vertical lines at the bottom of the chart represent *volume.*
59. The vertical lines in the circles, in relation to the price movements alone, are said to be *confirming.*
60. This is a *short-term* chart.

FIGURE 15

61. The pattern between points A and B is a *triangle.*
62. It is a *continuation* pattern.
63. The downturns at points C and D are both accompanied by *heavy volume.*

FIGURE 16

64. If the line at the bottom of the chart follows prices, it is said to *confirm* the price movements.

FIGURE 17

65. The line at the bottom of the chart represents the total number of *outstanding longs* or *shorts*.

66. At which point is new money—new buyers—coming into the market? *C*

67. At which point are contracts being liquidated as prices start to correct downward? *D*

FIGURE 18

68. Points A and B are called *blowoffs*.

69. If these patterns were to occur at market bottoms, they would be called *selling climaxes*.

70. During both patterns, volume was *heavy*.

71. During both patterns, open interest *declined*.

FIGURE 19

72. The chart is a *monthly* bar chart.

73. Long-term support can be found at roughly what level? *20*

74. Which point(s) demonstrate(s) the support level? *A, D*

75. Which point indicates the start of a major new trend? *E*

FIGURE 20

76. The two moving average lines represent an averaging of *price* data.

77. The 10 Day Average is said to be *shorter* than the 50 Day Average.

78. The *10 Day Average* signaled the market upturn first.

79. The *10 Day Average* gave a premature buy signal before the upturn.

FIGURE 21

80. Point(s) *B, D* demonstrate(s) the double crossover method.

81. Point *B* is a sell signal.

82. Point *D* is a buy signal.

FIGURE 22

83. The curve at the bottom of the chart is a(n) *oscillator.*

84. In range *A,* this market is said to be overbought.

85. In range *C,* this market is said to be oversold.

FIGURE 23

86. The horizontal line running through the oscillator at the bottom of the chart is called the *zero line.*

87. Point A, a crossing above the line, is a *buy* signal.

88. Point B, a crossing below the line, is a *sell* signal.

FIGURE 24

89. The RSI line represents a ratio determined by dividing the *up average* by the *down average.*

90. The chart demonstrates a *bottom* failure swing.

91. Point *C* signals a bottom.

FIGURE 25

92. In this chart, each box is equal to *.5.*

93. The reversal criterion is *3.*

94. Buy signals occur at point(s) *B, D, F.*

95. Sell signals occur at point(s) *A, C, E.*

96. If the reversal criterion were increased, the chart would be *less* sensitive to price movements.

FIGURE 26

97. The close price is found at point *B.*

98. When the close price is lower than the open price, the candlestick used would look like *F.*

99. The body is represented by *G.*

100. The shadow (wick or hair) is shown by *H.*

101. Long Days are reflected by *I.*